WILD FLOWERS OF CANADA

IMPRESSIONS AND SKETCHES OF A FIELD ARTIST

WILD FLOWERS OF CANADA

MOLLY LAMB BOBAK

Pagurian Press Limited
TORONTO

ISBN 0-88932-077-2
Printed and bound in Canada

Contents

To
Barbara

Foreword

This book is a double self-portrait. In it, Molly Lamb Bobak, a cherished friend to so many, writes about her life as a child, as an art student, and as an artist who has lived and worked in various parts of Canada and abroad.

Her narrative has a refreshing directness, for she has seen people, events, and places with sympathy and wonder. She expresses an innocence and an exuberance which is infectious and good humoured. She makes one wish that more artists would write about their experiences and their ways of looking at the world.

As with most artists, Molly's life is one of considerable intensity. She can be as engaged with people, or a walk in town or country, or the preparations for a meal as she is with painting. She allows herself to be constantly surprised by common ordinary things, and it is this attitude to being alive that makes her story worth reading.

The flower paintings are also self-portraits, though it may seem odd to say so. Flowers are symbolic parallels to human lives. For all their hardiness, they are vulnerable and delicate. They are wild and chaotic, yet they preserve pattern and order. They are sometimes plain and sometimes exotic, and they are as numerous and varied as humans themselves. Their brief and transitory lives are splendid, a raiment more glorious than Solomon's. William Blake could see "Heaven in a Wild Flower," and so have all artists and poets before him and since.

Flowers have always been a favourite subject for painters. David Milne, one of Molly's art heroes, felt that flowers were much like artists: both are radiant and useless. Both exist for no other purpose than to give grace to life, to provide aesthetic pleasure — a thrill and a joy that illuminate and enrich our lives. Neither contributes to the bare necessities of existence, but both endow life with meaning and dignity.

Molly's paintings of flowers have formal qualities which are striking. Her subjects in this book are mostly wild flowers, vibrant clusters floating in large white spaces like galaxies of colour in a universe of their own. The paintings are at once meticulous and spontaneous. They have a consuming vitality which their delicacy does not diminish. They have a balance which their seeming disorder does not destroy. They have an immediacy of vision which is constantly renewed with each viewing. They are an act of love.

Since Molly's life and Molly's paintings have already given such immense pleasure to those who know her and her work, the appearance of this book will help some of us to recover and to preserve valued memories. For those who have yet to meet Molly and her paintings, what better introduction could there be?

David P. Silcox
Toronto, March, 1978

Introduction

Molly Bobak is so much a person it is essential to insist that she is first of all a painter. Art is her life and her expression. Her oils of people in crowds suggest an expansive, even extrovert, spirit. Life is celebrated as a carnival — the pulse of life is beating, the game is being played, the drama is enacted. Yet her art is not one thing at all, nor is this artist that easily defined. Her watercolours of flowers show another world. It may be that the flowers fill the space as boisterously as the figures in crowds, but the spirit is different. It is inwardly directed towards quietness, introspection, and tenderness. The flowers vibrate with their own life. There is no anthropomorphism, hence no sentimentality or mere charm. Another spirit than what is human shines from these sumptuous yet fragile papers; the spirit of the plant itself independent of its reception by human eyes. The flowers speak for themselves, so I will say a word on the space they inhabit. It is mostly white paper, but it carries the coolness of the air, the movement of wind, the perfume of the flowers, and the jostling and urgency of their growth. Or, it is a spiritual element where our eyes can contemplate the impalpable and see the unseen. There is a quality of independence, as if the personality of the artist has not intruded. That is the miracle of these works—that they exist in their own world and seem hardly touched by the artist.

Yet Molly Lamb seems to be all personality. Her life is lived in a sort of turbulence of action, talk, laughter, and work. So vibrating is her presence that it is hard to imagine its retreat into the silence of creation and contemplation. One does not appreciate this artist by her work alone if one knows the person, one who colours the life of her friends and her community. Yet these flol live quite apart from the vibrations of the artist's being, as if they had grown fresh from the ground into the unclouded space of a pristine world.

Joe Plaskett
Paris, August 1977

Memories

On the following pages I shall try to capture the flavour of my life and hope that my words and my paintings will somehow add up to the same experience. I'll start by reminiscing about my childhood a long time ago in Burnaby Lake.

I remember a big yellow dahlia at the bottom of our garden—I can't think why, as I never cared for dahlias except for their acrid smell. And the skunk cabbages and the bog near the lake where the cows grazed. That was a smell to stay with you! Certain images never get lost—for example, the graceful sour cherry tree near our back door where the mint grew. Once, when digging in the earth beneath that tree, I found the fragments of a celluloid kewpie doll and by the coal bin in the basement the dusty remains of little green leggings I had outgrown, and I felt full of unexplained regret.

I remember the winter frost that raised the earth in muddy crystals and a frozen field mouse I saw one morning on my way to Miss Harry's kindergarten. Miss Harry's was the only school I ever liked, not counting art school. Miss Harry and her sister, Miss Woodward, also ran the post office in their house. I remember the wooden counter with one of those little bells people used to bang to get service and the small wire cage at the end where the stamps and the money were kept.

Our schoolroom was behind the counter—four low tables and four low chairs at each table. It was very dark and I wonder now what we did there. I can only remember playing with wooden blocks covered with shiny pictures of Humpty Dumpty, which I kept putting together over and over again.

Miss Harry was badly crippled. She wore heavy iron braces on her legs and had crutches to drag herself around with. Miss Woodward, on the other hand, held herself very straight and always wore Fair Isles cardigans and white dickeys.

I have a vague memory of their parlour—white lace curtains, green ferns on stands, cups in the cabinet, and Miss Woodward standing in the middle of the room with her dickey out of place. And with one huge downy pink breast exposed!

I remember when Miss Harry was kind to a new boy. He was crying and she gave him a Father Christmas decal off a Christmas cracker. It was shiny and strange and he stuck it on his cold red knee and stared at it. I'll bet it was from England. We were all English in those days in Burnaby Lake without, of course, realizing it. All, that is, except the vegetable man who was Chinese and the wood man who was a Hindu. The vegetable man didn't come to us because of our big garden, but he used to chug along very slowly in his black model-T truck with the wooden runners along each side so you could get up and pick your vegetables. He grew them on Lulu Island in perfectly straight lines in the rich loam by the Fraser River.

How much space we had! Meadows, woods, tangled gardens, streams, ponds—and, of course, the deserted old Mervin house, with its dark weathered wood and broken windows. Did we really find a man lying on the floor there, dead or asleep? How about the crazy lady who talked to herself and fluttered transfers out the window of the Inter-Urban tram on the way to Vancouver? My brother Abby told me she had a child and had thrown him into Deer Lake to teach him to swim. There were water lilies on Deer Lake and transparent amber water smelling of reeds, and Oriental poppies growing in Miss Harry's garden on the edge of Deer Lake.

Years later when I was going to a convent school in Vancouver, our class was asked to tell a story with a moral ending. I told the one about the crazy lady throwing her child in the lake, but Sister Janet became so incensed, she told the whole class not to speak to Molly Lamb, the liar, for one whole week. Humiliated and ostracized, I couldn't understand the punishment since I loved my violent story and believed it. After all, I had seen the crazy lady.

There was also the lady with the hundred pockets who appeared every year at Miss Harry's summer fete. Her dress, a dull pink, came down to her ankles with rows and rows of pockets. Every pocket held a present which we could buy for five or ten cents.

There were so many fetes in those days. Fetes or plays or parties. Then there was Miss Den Peel. She used to sing contralto in Gilbert and Sullivan performances in New Westminster, and she was a Commissioner in the Girl Guides, too. She often produced plays in her garden. I remember "Alice in Wonderland" in which I was a card and had to stand still for a long time.

But it's the winter plays and parties I remember best. Molly Lamb and Barbara Biart, full of fun are they. In each other's ears they tell secrets every day. My Anny has carried on the tradition. She writes her own material, and one Christmas when she was thirteen she and a neighbour's daughter produced a chess game play in our living room. I noticed that the only thing that had changed since our day was the language. One line I remember well, "You took my castle, you dirty asshole."

My mother used to dress us in green caps and fern fronds to open the door for Christmas carolers. And Mrs. Pears, who seemed so old, would do her trick of wearing a great long coat, turning her back to the audience, and, as if by magic, start growing taller until she reached the face of the grandfather clock. I think she did it by raising her walking stick up her back into her large hat. But I really don't want to know. How hard our mothers worked to make all those costumes and do the chores as well! Growing vegetables, cleaning chickens, throwing damp tea leaves on the rug to make the sweeping less dusty, keeping milk cool under muslin cloths.

My mother often had grown-up parties when Dad went to the Session in Victoria. I never asked what the Session was, but of course it was the sitting of the Provincial Legislature, and I suppose my father had to present some sort of papers about mining in British Columbia because he was the Secretary of the Mining Association. Mum would invite her friends from Vancouver to stay for the weekend −Mr. George Parker, Mrs. Dorothy, Mrs. Grace, Mrs. Ethyl, Uncle Stu, Mr. Tim Cole. I used to call them that, as a sign of respect, I suppose. They'd come on a Friday night on the Inter-Urban and get off at Rayside Station −that little red house with the wooden platform and the smell of urine inside and all the initials carved on the walls. I was never at these parties but I could always hear the din from upstairs. They didn't drink much in those days, just a bit of homemade beer, but they sang and danced.

Once Uncle Stu rolled in the old Beatty washer which was made of wood −like a half barrel −and Uncle Bill went outside to the rabbit hutch and brought in a couple of rabbits and did magic tricks with the washing machine. I also remember a sleety February morning when all the party friends were in bed, four women in my dad's fourposter, and Uncle Bill gave a false alarm that Dad was coming home from the Session in Victoria and was already walking up Rayside Avenue. I was in the long narrow hall upstairs and I remember seeing the women in their horrid rayon nighties rushing towards me out of his bedroom, tin boxes of cigarettes scattering across the hall.

That Uncle Bill −I never liked him although he worked hard for us and kept the chickens and rabbits and cows. I think he drank. One night he climbed up on the McNairs' roof and put a stuffed owl in their chimney; another time his red setter, Nick, got into the chickenhouse and killed two hundred chickens. That was the first time I saw a man cry.

Mrs. Dorothy and Mrs. Grace once lived in Fredericton, and that's how my mother met them. She answered an ad in an English paper for a mother's help in Canada, which had been put in by the Ross Thompson family who lived in a big house on the corner of Regent and Charlotte. The family had eleven children and Mrs. Dorothy and Mrs. Grace were two of them, although almost my mother's age.

Roots

When I was small my mother told me many stories about New Brunswick, and like all good stories they didn't need dates or facts, just atmosphere. How she drove in a sleigh from Oromocto to Fredericton on the frozen Saint John River, and it was so cold she had to hold two hot potatoes in her mittened hands to keep warm. How once just before leaving New Brunswick, she met a hermit in the woods, and he gave her a present and told her not to open it until she arrived in Montreal —she did as she was told but left the parcel on the train, unopened. How she sang in the cathedral and broke into tears once when she sang a solo in a requiem for two young men who had been killed in the Battle of Jutland. She sold vegetables, too, outside the City Hall and then she'd go to Barker House and have a great big dinner on the proceeds. Oh, how she loved New Brunswick! When by chance we happened to settle here in 1960, it took me a little while to separate her myths and images from my own love of the place.

She always moved on, my mother. After being with the Thompsons for a while, she answered another ad to look after a garden in St. Andrews. She told me stories of the high Fundy tides, and of one night when a man and his team of horses coming across the spit from Minister's Island to the mainland were caught in a fast tidewater. Before they drowned, everyone could hear their fearful cries.

In St. Andrews she worked for an architect, Mr. Maxwell, and his family. A little while ago when I was teaching a summer course in St. Andrews, who should be in my class but the Maxwell daughter, who must have been fourteen or so when my mother worked for her family! She took me to the beautiful house her father had built and I saw the lawns my mother mowed so long ago. She told me that when her father had interviewed Mum for the job, he had expected to see a young man because she had signed her letter "A. S. Price." At first he refused to hire her. But she hit him on the arm, well, not really hit, but made some sort of gesture of strength, and said, "I can do anything." And so she was hired.

St. Andrews was a summer place for wealthy Montreal families. They built magnificent houses and every summer they came down on the train with their mountains of luggage and many servants. Some still come back −like the Maxwell girl, although of course it isn't the same any more.

Well, my mother decided to go back to Montreal with the Maxwells. She rented a room from them and started a hand laundry for the rich. She washed their silks and satins and delivered them in an old black baby carriage. She told me that once while wheeling her pram along Sherbrooke Street a gust of wind caught her laundry, whisked it into the air, and deposited somebody's pair of silk pyjamas on a telephone wire, where it waved like a banner.

Although she delivered laundry to the back doors of Westmount, she met some of her clients socially; I guess because she was so friendly with the Maxwells. It was around this time that she met my father. Did she do his laundry or did she meet him at a party? I don't know.

He had come to British Columbia from England when he was sixteen. The CPR had just reached Port Moody, so Dad headed there. He was hired by a farmer, a Mr. Agassiz, to work on his farm. Dad always said he had had to work so hard as a boy that it had stunted his growth, but I think he just wasn't a tall man. He must have been ambitious though. He started a newspaper in Chilliwack, and he was also a lay reader in the Anglican Church. I am vague about his life, as well as my mother's. I do know he married young, a pretty girl from Greenwood in the Kettle Valley, and they had six children. Two of the girls died very young, although the younger one lived until she was ten. Her name was Dolly and she was painted by Sophie Pemberton, an artist accomplished in a traditional way − not a maverick like Emily Carr but, just the same, a sensitive painter. What she could do with whites! In her portrait of Dolly, the little girl is wearing a wide-brimmed soft hat. Such tender changes of white, and under it a dear little face framed in dark gold hair. When Dolly died of measles, Dad was crushed. He never felt quite the same affection for his four sons, at least I don't think he did.

When I was small I don't remember him being around very much except when he photographed us in the garden. That huge camera on a tripod and an accordion thing and a bulb that hung down for pressing the shutter, and Dad under a black cloth reaching out with one arm to slip a plate down somewhere while we had to stand naked and still, pretending to be interested in the glittering crepe paper butterfly he'd clipped on a real flower. How long it took!

We didn't become friends, Dad and I, until after I had grown up. Then we had much in common, both being painters. He was more romantic than I and he used to say, "Painting is love."

Long before I was born he rose high in the Canadian Mining Association, and that's how he came to live in Montreal. By this time he had already amassed a modest but interesting collection of paintings and pots and rugs and Buddhas, and had met A. Y.

GERANIUMS

My mother never cared much for geraniums —she planted phlox and night-scented stock and asters and mignonette. I first came to love geraniums after seeing them in a Cezanne painting —he did a few on a window ledge in those simple earthenware flower pots which the French still make. I love to paint geraniums because of their awkward changes in direction —they suggest interesting arrangements in space —staccato rhythms instead of undulating, obvious ones.

14

MOLLY LAMB B

Jackson and Arthur Lismer and Frederick Varley and Jock MacDonald. He became their friend and champion. His life was rich and full, but it wasn't shared by his wife, who could not cope with their new life in Montreal. She wasn't well and was, perhaps, being a simple person, bewildered by her changed status. Dad needed a housekeeper, which is when Mum moved in and took over the household.

Then Dad had a nervous breakdown, and the whole family moved from Montreal back to the West to Burnaby Lake, where he got well by ploughing the fields and taking a simpler job, still with the Mining Association.

I remember my father's wife. I called her "Gombo," a silly form of godmother. I remember her sitting in her wicker chair, and once in a hurry bringing her a cup of tea in a pale willow pattern cup which I dropped, splashing the tea all over her. I remember how she consoled me. She was not capable of doing much, but some Sundays she went to St. James' Anglican Church in Vancouver and sometimes to Chinatown.

I think she resented my mother although she needed her, and always pretended she was a servant. Once Gombo invited two Anglican priests from the St. James' Church to tea, and as Mum served them, using my father's best silver teapot and good china, she overheard Gombo's aside to the priests: "I prefer yellow help, you know, but you can't get it any more." As time went on Gombo withdrew more and more. She slept in a little room with a reproduction of Leonardo's Christ above her bed, and she sang hymns to herself. Willoughby —I called him Abby —Gombo's youngest son and my dearest half-brother, was very good to her right until she died.

My father and mother weren't very close, either, and they pretty much went their separate ways. Mum had a habit of sneaking into his bedroom and going through his trouser pockets looking for change, which was a game they played. When we lived in Burnaby Lake Mum sometimes went to Vancouver to see the British Guild Players at the old Empress Theatre on Hastings Street. That was my favourite time —Saturday night — because Abby would whip up the jersey's cream —her name was Molly too —and put pineapple into it, and I'd sit on his lap and he'd read me wonderful stories about a prissy English girl and the Katzenjammer Kids and Maggie and Jiggs.

Growing Up

Later on when we lived on 54th Avenue, Abby went to the University to become a parson, but he always had time to help in our big garden and milk the cow. In the early evening we'd go down to 57th where we pastured her with my donkey Alice, and bring them both up to Oak Street to the barn. I also went there to roller skate because it was the only piece of paved road in the district.

At 54th we had many visitors and a lot of people who stayed with us for long periods: children whose parents couldn't cope with them, a would-be actor who finally made it during the war in London, a huge lonely American woman who hated Mum's cooking. How did *she* happen to stay with us, I wonder? My father disapproved of these visitors, although they were only there one at a time. To get away from them, he had a studio built as a wing on the far side of the house where he could be alone.

He welcomed only one visitor, as far as I can remember. This was during the early part of the War when people in England feared an invasion. Have you ever heard of Roger Fry? He was an art critic, writer, and painter. He had a daughter Pamela who had three children, and whose husband was a dear fellow, a Romanian Jew called Mic. He was worried about the three children because of their being half Jewish, and decided Pamela should bring them out to British Columbia where she had a brother who had a ranch in the interior. They came, but it wasn't easy living with relatives, so Pamela moved to Vancouver, wondering what to do next. She was staying at the Devonshire Hotel when my art school teacher, Jack Shadbolt, met her and steered her to us.

Pamela's two older children went to a private school in Victoria, but her little boy Roger stayed with us too. Pamela parted her hair in the middle, wore peasant clothes and sandals, and looked like Virginia Woolf. Roger was a beautiful boy with curly chestnut hair, olive skin, dark eyes, and a stalky little body. He was bright and precocious. Pamela was modern and Roger was allowed to be natural in his habits. That's the first thing that put Dad off – the kid would fart in his studio. But he loved Pamela. They talked about art and she allowed him to hang her Renoir portrait above his fireplace. He loved that. Roger, however, had to be kept away from Dad

BOUQUET WITH TOBACCO PLANT

When I was young my father had a collection of valuable Oriental pots and vases, and one from the Ming Dynasty was particularly rare. It was pure white and stood on three legs. My mother loved the vases but always wanted to fill them with flowers or branches of apple or cherry blossoms, which bothered my father. Now I have much more ordinary vases, but I always fill them with flowers too. My mother never made flower arrangements —she simply put things together; maybe that's why I have such an aversion to florists' bouquets with their bows, coloured sprays, and wired pompoms.

18

Molly Lamb B

Pamela believed in natural foods, and she had drilled Roger into the habit of eating raw, organic carrots rather than chocolate bars or candies. Once when Dad, particularly surly, was sitting in his armchair looking sour, the little boy went up to him, put his hand on Dad's knee, and said in his impeccable English accent, "The trouble with you Mr. Lamb, is that you eat too much starch."

Our place on 54th Avenue had two acres of ground. There was a stucco cottage at the beginning of the dirt driveway which we rented; the main house was at the end of this drive. There were poplar trees and a Gravenstein apple tree. Also cherries, chestnuts, pears, and a vegetable garden beside the barn where we kept the cow and the donkey. The house rambled. It had a stone terrace in front and steps leading down to flower gardens and a tennis court, and it was my job to roll that grass court with a heavy iron roller, while Abby marked the lines with a gadget that held whitewash in a pan. There was a wheel on each end with a canvas band that went around the wheels through the can and left a white line on the grass.

Every Sunday all the people who used to come to Burnaby Lake would now arrive for tennis. Mum would have made a huge tea —eclairs, cakes, sandwiches, a big jug of milk, and a bigger teapot of Nabob orange pekoe tea. Everyone wore whites and sat on the lawn beside a trellis of Dorothy Perkins roses, those little pink climbers that last all summer long. When Emma, our pet bulldog, had pups they were brought out for everyone to admire.

Dad had friends, too. When we lived in Burnaby Lake, A. Y. Jackson periodically came to see us. My mother said Jackson used to wear a pair of shoes he was very proud of, but the soles held a lot of mud, and Mum didn't think too much of them. We also had visits from Frederick Varley, who lived in Vancouver then with his family in a dark house with leaded windows and overhanging vines. Once Mrs. Varley had us to tea and I remember she had burned the rock cakes. They came to see us at Burnaby Lake too. I liked one of their sons, Peter, who wore big black boots and kicked at the water butt by the barn.

Mr. Varley hated kids. He flicked his hand whenever I got too close, but when I grew up he used to pat me.

Dad had other friends. There was an architect called Sam McClure, and, of course, he knew Emily Carr. She never visited him, but when he went to Victoria he saw her often. He and Marius Barbeau, the anthropologist, were responsible for getting Emily her first major show at the National Gallery. Dad and Emily got on very well, for a time at least. He bought a lot of her work before the Montreal dealers had ever heard of her, but later on when Dad felt he had too many Emily Carrs, he sold some of them at a profit. She found out and it ended the friendship. He did a lot for her, though, and it's a pity she got so angry. The famous photograph of Emily in her skullcap, leaning forward on her arms, was taken by Dad

I met her once. She was having a large exhibition in the Vancouver Art Gallery when I was in my second year at the art school. I had just painted my first oil, very French Impressionist, and I went to the gallery to show it to her, but at the last minute I got cold feet and, instead, put my painting in the women's washroom and just had a chat.

For my father the significant summer occurred in the middle 1930s. The art school organized a painting holiday on Savary Island, and he went along with the staff and students on an old union steamship, probably the *Lady Cynthia*. I don't believe he ever had a better time in his life. He took some impromptu painting lessons from Fred Amess that great, kindhearted, bumbling man who had been Varley's student and later became a teacher and principal of the Vancouver School of Art.

From that time on Dad never stopped painting his joyful gardens and fantasies. He would put a canvas on his easel, sit in his armchair, chain-smoke, contemplate for some time, then walk to the canvas and nervously put a dab of paint somewhere he felt it belonged — sometimes even a series of small strokes, no, not strokes — nervous dabs. Painting became his chief pleasure and his great love.

TULIPS

Tulips remind me of elementary school windows in May. I can still smell the paste we used which came in a small glass bottle with a tin-handled brush with coarse black hair. I wonder, do children still use the same paste to stick their paper tulips on to classroom windows?

In the autumn we pot bulbs to tide us through the long cold winter. These tulips were on my kitchen table for a long time before they became tired and started to fade —it seemed to me they were very beautiful in their old age so I painted them just before they died —fragile, thin, and dignified.

22

MOLLY LAMB B

Art School

Varley, Jock MacDonald, and another man whose name I forget broke away from the Vancouver School of Art and started their own place on Georgia Street. They called it the "British Columbia College of Art" and some of the students from the Vancouver School of Art went with them.

Their most promising student was Vera Weatherby. I remember a photograph of Vera then. She was tiny-boned and had almond-shaped eyes and a delicately pursed mouth, also a little downy moustache, but not a dark or ugly one. I did not know her then but later she often came to our house. She was shy and beautiful and moved with a grace that made me think of a Japanese tea ceremony. They say Varley was the sort of teacher you either totally followed or totally rejected. Vera was one of the followers. Everyone knows now that Varley left his family and moved up the mountain to a studio high in Lynn Valley, and Vera, primly brought-up Vera, went with him. It was here he painted many of the Vera portraits and the North Vancouver ferry at night and the "Dharana" – that was Vera too.

I never asked her anything about that time, but I know Vancouver society was hard on her, especially after Varley left to go east. She must have felt very much alone then, but Dad remained a friend and admirer of her work and even supplied her with a studio and materials during the late 1930s. Later on he asked her to paint my portrait. It was good, but more like Vera's gentle character than mine. I was a plumpish kid then with untidy hair, peasant clothes, sad moods, dizzy heights, big eating sessions, but Vera painted me quiet, with no flying ribbons.

I was at the art school then. The first year I did nothing. Art bored me, although, like most children, I had drawn and painted all my life. I felt there was no hope for me as a painter, because I had been told so by my teachers. I became apathetic and distracted and loved the theatre, or thought I did. In fact, I once even auditioned at CJOR radio for the part of Tom Sawyer's aunt – I was auditioned by Bernie Braden and John Drainie. Of course I didn't get it. Too English, too young, too little training.

I didn't want to go back to art school, but since I had not finished school my mother, a firm believer in finishing what one began, forced me back for the second year.

On the first day back at the old red brick building on Cambie and Dunsmuir streets, I met the new teacher, Jack Shadbolt. First, he set the class to drawing each other. I did my usual dull, unobservant work of a classmate called Eileen, and waited in dread for Shadbolt to pull it to shreds. To my astonishment, he didn't. Instead, he showed me how to improve it. He even said it had a strong line. His encouragement meant a lot to me. Anything could happen from then on; anything was possible with a little skill and a lot of work – Shadbolt introduced me to a great world.

As a little girl I had loved to look at two big old books of my dad's by Honoré Daumier. I couldn't read the text, but I understood the satire of the drawings. I also loved an English illustrator called Rackham, who did meticulous drawings of children in the woods being almost clutched by great gnarled trees. Some of the children wore leather gaiters.

But Shadbolt showed us Cezanne. What Cezanne could do with an apple or a glass decanter! One could see layers of watercolour over surfaces and taut blue strokes shattering around the edges, open, moving. Suddenly you weren't looking at apples or decanters any more, but painting. I almost went crazy.

Shadbolt often came to our house right after school. He and I would get on the old Number 17 streetcar at Hastings and Cambie, but if we got a seat, it would never be together as it was always crowded at that time of the day. As we neared 54th and Oak people would begin to get off and often I'd have an empty place beside me. I'd move over to the window and hope that Shadbolt would come over and sit next to me, but he never did. As soon as we got to our house he would begin to draw everything and everyone – my brother Abby, Emma the dog, Dad's teapot with pears around it. His energy was amazing.

Once Dad let Shadbolt do a mural for the far end of his studio, but that turned out badly. When it was unveiled, Dad hated it. The mural had a Chinese theme, with Mum a big nude Buddha and Dad a mean-looking old mandarin. I forget the rest, but Dad didn't find it funny and it ended up in the barn.

Those were the early war years, and I remember a famous English musician and conductor who came to Vancouver for the duration, as they used to say. His name was Arthur Benjamin. His portly mother came with him, also a young Canadian painter, Eric Friefield, who had had some early success in London with his brilliant wet watercolours. Friefield was broke and needed a place to stay, so he came to live with us. We became great friends and I learned a lot from him. Often we talked and painted together. Eventually he joined the army and I didn't meet him again until years later in Toronto. He is and was one of those rare private painters who went his own way – no trendy style for him although he knew very well what was going on in the international art world. He chose his own heroes and remained independent; a meticulous draftsman with a limited output compared to his friend Shadbolt.

But to get back to Arthur Benjamin and his mother. Arthur Benjamin had become a local celebrity, conducting promenade concerts in the old wooden Coliseum near

MORNING GLORY

There is something Art Nouveau about the morning glory, and its shapes are forever associated in my mind with that fashion. It grows wild on the river banks and tame in our garden, where it first climbs formally to the top of the fence, then falls gracefully as if suspended in air. I like that feeling of space, and, although morning glories are such neat and organized flowers, I like to paint them.

MOLLY LAMB B

Burrard and Davie streets. I went to all the concerts; they were a great thing for Vancouver, very popular and always crowded. One Sunday Benjamin and his mother came to tea, and even Dad joined us on the terrace. Tea was my mother's usual seedcake and plumcake. She always made a big batter, divided it in half, put raisins and currants in one and caraway seeds in the other, sprinkled sugar on top of both, and baked them in bread pans.

She had just made a batch of bread that day and after the tea the Benjamins came into the house to see our Emily Carrs and Varleys and Lismers and Chinese pots and Buddhas and other things. Well, since Mrs. Benjamin had a hard time walking because of her weight, it was decided she should leave by the back door. Our house had a kitchen on two levels, but you had to step up or down to almost every other room too and the narrow porch at the back was no exception. Mum had put her fresh bread to cool on the counter beside the door. Just as Mrs. Benjamin was leaving, she turned to exclaim about the beautiful loaves of bread and missed the step. Down she went and became wedged into that narrow space. The poor woman was in agony. She had broken her kneecaps or something equally awful and Arthur was in a panic.

Mum fetched a mattress and yelled to Dad, "Harold, get some brandy, for heaven's sake!"

Dad reluctantly unlocked his liquor cabinet and Mum rushed a glass to Mrs. Benjamin. Arthur, who was bending over her saying things like, "Speak to me Mother," took the brandy and downed it at one gulp.

Eventually we managed to get Mrs. Benjamin onto a mattress and out the back door. We even called an ambulance and off she went to the hospital. We sent flowers and apologies but never saw them again.

Breakup

By 1942 our household was breaking up. Abby had long gone, married, and with a parish. I was working at Hill's Yellowpoint Lodge on Vancouver Island that summer, and Mum was getting itchy feet. Dad asked her to marry him, but she refused. Instead, he bought her a waterfront summer resort called Arbutus Point on Galiano Island. They went over to the island together and found the property—about forty acres, a sandy beach, two bays, two houses, and a long point jutting out to Active Pass. The houses were furnished and in good shape, and there was a barn and a long shed cut into cubicles and used as rustic bedrooms for summer guests. Budlea and long-stalked white poppies grew outside the shed and there were apple trees and a place for a vegetable garden. And crushed clam shell paths. And the point, that was the best part—it was formed of that peculiar Gulf Island sandstone, smooth, light coloured. Covered with moss and grass, very green in spring and bleached gold in autumn, rock flowers grew low on it—wild blue lobelia and pink bell things and there were little dark pools filled by rain or high tide water. One could find the dried shells of sea urchins there. On the far side the smooth stone moved into the sea. On the other side the tide had worn away the stone and made undulating caves. Wonderful in nature, too obvious in art! All this for seven thousand dollars.

"Harold," said Mum, "You must get married again." He thought it an excellent idea, took an old friend out to lunch at the Georgia Hotel, and proposed. That evening, when he came jerking up the drive in his Austin 10, Mum could hardly wait to hear the news. I remember him tugging his goatee and giving a nervous little laugh. "She refused me," he said. Mum suggested he try Vera. At first he couldn't conceive of her accepting him. They were friends, but so far apart in ages—she in her early thirties, he in his late sixties.

I knew about these plans, but I was working hard at Yellowpoint Lodge and didn't give them much thought.

One day, late in the summer, I got a day off and went down to Nanaimo, took the *Princess Elaine* down to Vancouver, then the old Number 17 streetcar. Up our drive in the dusk. The sun was sending its last dappled patches of cool light through the lovely Lombardy poplar outside the back door. When I tried the door, it was locked. Mum never locked the door, and I knew something was up. I saw that a kitchen window was

COSMOS

I remember cosmos against the stone wall in our garden in Vancouver. We had a grass tennis court and friends came to play every summer weekend. My mother made tea in a big pot and brown bread sandwiches and plum cake. There was milk from our cow in a willow pattern jug and the men wore white flannel pants. I loved to get up early in the morning and roll the court before the dew left it. The roller was heavy and as I went up and down it made two swatches of different tones of green.

Here in New Brunswick every small farm has a random bed of cosmos somewhere between the battery of high bird houses (for the purple martins) and the whirling bleach bottles.

Bruno grows cosmos, and I love to paint them. In the fall I race against the first killing frost to put down all they suggest to me. I have an old brush with a few hairs left in it which helps me say something about the elegance of these crisp-growing fronds.

30

MOIIY LAMB B

open so I climbed up to it and let myself in by crawling onto the old organ which was at the far end of the kitchen, flush with the windows. It was dark and I must have made quite a commotion because I'd hardly jumped to the floor when Dad appeared, coming slowly through the hall with another figure close behind him.

"Dad," I said, peering at him, "You shaved off your beard!"

"Moll," he said, "I was married today."

"To Miss so and so?" I blurted. The name of the first lady.

"No," said a small voice behind Dad, "To me. Do you mind?"

It was Vera.

We all hugged each other and had a little talk, and I went up to my old bedroom and cried. Not because of the marriage, but because our old life was over. As for Dad and Vera, that was the beginning of a long and happy life together, and for Mum too.

Their relationship was cordial, although Mum felt a little, what shall I say, afraid isn't the word — guilty perhaps. When she moved to Galiano she had taken a few things with her, among them a small oil sketch by A. Y. Jackson. Dad never forgot what he had in his collection — he valued everything he had. Mum did not — she swapped the A. Y. for an ordinary French Canadian hooked wallhanging, which, when washed, ran together and was ruined. Much later, in the 1950s, Dad wrote and asked her for the painting.

I was on the island at the time, and she said to me, "What am I going to do? I've swapped the damn thing!"

"Well," I said, "I'll write to A. Y., explain the whole thing — he doesn't value owning things either — he'll understand, and I'll buy another winter scene from him. Dad won't know the difference after all these years."

Jackson enjoyed being in on our scheme and sent me a sketch saying he'd never given me a wedding present — he'd been at my Polish wedding party in Toronto — and now he was sending the sketch as a wedding present. Mum sent it to Dad, who never said a word.

One afternoon years later when I was visiting him and Vera, he asked me how it was he had received a Jackson sketch dated 1954 when Mum had taken his dated in the 1920s. I told him the story. He shook his head, chuckled, and got a bit furious. Then he gave me the painting, and it's now hanging upstairs in our house.

Island Life

Mum was never a business woman. She ran Arbutus Point as a summer resort, but found it difficult to charge her guests. She hired no help and did all her cooking on a Canada Pride wood stove. The guests used to make their own beds and lay the tables and even peel vegetables, and if there were any little boys in the group, she turned them into waiters. Most of her clients were friends anyway, or they became friends, but occasionally someone arrived who didn't like her unorthodox approach — one rather spoiled lady in particular.

Mum was orderly and clean. She used to get up at five in the morning to empty the outhouse cans into a pit in the woods, then she'd sprinkle them liberally with chlorate of lime. Then she'd go for a swim, light the fire, and start breakfast. One early dawn she was doing her routine jobs and had just opened the flap behind the outhouse to pull out the cans, when she heard a refined but panicky voice saying, "One moment, please."

The summers were hectic. When fall came the resort closed and the island became peaceful. In the evenings Mum could go to Mary Anne Point to visit Paul Scoones, who had once taught mathematics at Eton and who had something called a Davis gramophone with a huge horn and a big collection of records. He had built his house on a rock overlooking Active Pass and you could sit in his living room with the light of an oil lamp, listen to his music, and watch the lights of the boats as they went through the narrow pass. Sometimes the moon shone on the water and sometimes just the stars were out.

Up the road from Arbutus Point was the general store run by Mr. Fred and Mr. Joe Burrill — two bachelors who had come from Yorkshire many, many years ago. Mr. Fred cooked and gardened; Mr. Joe was in charge of the store, and he also played the piano. They wore sleeveless sweaters and peaked caps and were contented people.

One day one of Mum's summer visitors had to buy some Kotex, and, like most people in those days, she was embarrassed to ask for it, especially from an old bachelor. She gathered her courage and went into the store, but came out defeated. Mr. Joe had sold her a little package of water glass solution for preserving eggs, and had told her that if she were careful she could use it twice!

33

A JUG OF AUGUST FLOWERS

Were I a horticulturalist I would write all sorts of interesting facts about flowers —and give them their proper names too —but alas, I am no scholar and have an impatient way of responding to life. I am content to leave detail and cataloguing to others, but when the colour and texture and shape of flowers come together in a white pot, their meaning is a visual delight —that's why it is hard to write about them. I hope they speak for themselves.

34

MOIIY LAMB B

The Burrills were dear friends of everyone. They rented a one-room cottage to another Yorkshire bachelor, Jack Kingsmill, who had done a little of everything, though mostly fishing. Jack was a gentle, humorous fellow and he and Mum eventually married.

Mum's great love was making gardens grow. All the years I knew her she'd work like a steer at her garden, bringing it to the point where she felt she could do no more, then moving to another likely piece of wild ground and beginning all over again. I know the feeling. It's like having a stack of new white canvasses, full of nothing but promise.

During those Galiano years Mum moved five or six times. More than that, because one year she and Jack actually left Galiano and became the caretakers of their friend's place on Hornby Island, a little farther north, which reminds me of the story of the horse in winter.

There was a law on Hornby Island which allowed the animals to run free. One bitterly cold day a group of horses broke into the property and did a lot of damage. Jack got his gun out and decided to scare them off. By mistake he hit one between the eyes, and it fell dead in the field. This was illegal and there was a heavy fine for shooting a horse, so Mum and Jack decided they'd better bury it as fast as they could. They worked far into the night, digging the hard ground to make a grave for it, and then again all the next day. By the time they had dug the hole big enough, the horse was stiff. Somehow they managed to roll the poor beast into the hole, but to their dismay its legs shot straight up to heaven. There was nothing for it but to saw them off.

I think it was incidents like these that made them yearn to be back on Galiano, and it wasn't long before they packed up their few belongings and returned. But I'm getting ahead of myself. There is more to say about the war years.

Army Days

After that summer at Yellowpoint I decided to join the army. I went to the old Vancouver Hotel which had been stripped bare of all its lavish trappings and was hollow and grey. I had a medical and signed papers all afternoon. When it was over the corporal showed me to my room. Bare, bare, bare —even a naked electric light bulb over the brown double bunk which was to be my bed – the top half. I wondered what I'd done. I decided to go out into the grey November air as fast as I could, but, to my horror, they wouldn't let me. I had to have a pass, and that was the most shocking thing of all. I finally managed to get one which allowed me to be out until 11 P.M.

Mum was in town and we arranged to meet at Scott's Café for supper. I was so upset I couldn't eat and that worried her because I was such a pig.

"We'll get you out," she said, "I'll write to Mackenzie King."

The idea comforted me that dreary evening, although I doubted if she could do anything.

Three days later I was so happy, nothing could have got me out of the army. I started to like both my roommates and the dishwashing job I had in the basement canteen, although we were made to wear hairnets and awful green uniforms. Still, it was something new and everyone was cheerful and pleasant.

After a month I was sent to Vermillion for basic training. We were taken in trucks to the CNR station on Main Street and given berths on the train. It was all supposed to be hush hush. It was the first time I had ever been to Alberta and had never felt real winter cold before.

We got out of the train in the bright clear morning at Vermillion and had to march to the barracks, but I had not yet been issued a new CWAC uniform, and was wearing a short tartan skirt, a sloppy Joe sweater, and bobby socks. My legs would have frozen had I marched to the barracks, so they put me in the staff car and I was driven to my new home in style.

By Christmas we of the Canadian Women's Army Corps were all good friends. It was as though we'd always lived together in this curious style: marching about with arms swinging, shining buttons, having drill, learning about VD and first aid and singing inane

FALL DAISIES

I *love to try to translate white flowers on white paper. The idea is to coax the flowers to emerge with the least tone one can use — just expose them as simply as possible.*

MOLLY LAMB B

songs. I remember "We're the Girls of the Army Corps You Heard So Much About," to the tune of "Eleven More Months and Eleven More Days." And another one, "Hitler, the CWACs Are on Their Way, Britain Expect Us Any Day, Good Girls Would Cut Off Our Curls and the Nazis the Blighters Will Pay," to the tune of "Colonel Bogey." It was all make-believe and yet happening.

I couldn't go home for Christmas – there wasn't time to get to Galiano Island, so I stayed in the almost deserted barracks, and it was probably the best Christmas I have ever had. The almost empty building, the mess hall where just a few of us had the traditional turkey dinner, the surreal night I was on fire picket and had to do the rounds at midnight. It was fifty-four below and dead still, a clear starry night, white smoke rising straight up in the air, and the snow squeaking under my ugly army galoshes. Little rests in the quiet kitchen, drinking tea with the cook.

Later, when I was stationed in the East, I did get home on furloughs. I'd come by train, sitting all the way drinking big cans of tomato juice and eating warm sardines in the summer heat as we crossed the prairies. Through the open windows specks of soot blew in on a hot, dry wind.

In Vancouver I'd take the *Princess Mary* across the cool sweet Gulf to Galiano and be in a fine garden again, and my mother would be sort of keening at the door wearing a fresh blue cotton dress from Eaton's catalogue. She'd have bowls of flowers in the house and would make me a salad of lettuce, chives, parsley, and mint. And the Burrills would have me to supper and Mr. Joe would play the Lorelei on the piano.

Later on in the 1960s I often went home to Galiano with Sasha and little Anny and sometimes Bruno. By then I was doing watercolours and once I painted a simple cabbage poppy which had seeded itself on the compost heap. Mum laughed because I'd chosen to paint something that had come up by chance. But that was the difference between us – I have never wanted to tend a garden; it's the rambling flowers that fascinate me. That's why I love New Brunswick so much – it's full of wild, hardy flowers. Mayflowers nestle under the snow if you scratch for them at the end of March, and bloodroot, white against the dark loam. Trout lilies, too. Later on towards the end of April spring suddenly bursts and flowers come tumbling out one after another with such speed it almost makes me dizzy with greed. Anemones, jacks-in-the-pulpit, trilliums, fiddleheads. Traditionally fiddleheads are eaten with a bony fish called shad or another fish called a gaspereau. Then there are ladies' slippers, sweet rocket, and on and on. After living in Fredericton for so long, I have all my places for looking and finding and every year these familiar experiences are fresh to me. This place is on an intimate scale a person can contain. Maritimers have always known it, of course. It shapes their way of life.

My friend David has land at Scotch Settlement about twenty-five miles from Fredericton, and last summer he and Ene, his friend, made trails through the maple woods and out into the meadows and back again where the fir trees grow, covered now with scallops of snow. I took my shirt off and felt the sun on my back. Sometimes when there's a full moon we go out at night and ski through the woods with their long blue shadows and silence. But once there was a wild wind and the clouds came up and made a blizzard and suddenly we were shrouded in dark white. We couldn't even see each other. And, just as suddenly, the storm subsided and the moon shot out from a bank of orange black into the sky like a flung frisbee.

Back to the army days in 1942. I made a personal discovery that everyone in the army was wonderful. Really, I did believe that. It was a comfort to understand that basically we are all alike. Maybe the CWAC uniform had something to do with it, or all that marching we had to do together. Oh, there were a few odd ones, like a big tough CWAC we called Timber because she had been a logger. At mealtimes, the orderly officer would come in to the mess hall and a sergeant would blow a whistle and shout, "Any complaints?"

Timber would bawl back, "Yes Ma'am, there's too much saltpetre in this ham."

And the rest of us would all giggle and smirk, because, as Candy Melynchuk said, "Everyone knows saltpetre doesn't do a thing to girls."

After two months in Vermillion I was sent to a non-commissioned officers' school in St. Anne de Bellevue, outside Montreal. I wasn't NCO material so I was shipped back to Vancouver to wait and see what they'd do with me; all the time I was writing and drawing a daily diary of life in the army. Finally, because I was classified as an artist, they decided to send me to a drafting course in Toronto. Little did they know I couldn't draw a straight line!

Apart from the course, I loved Toronto. On my walks after classes I discovered places like the Kensington Market, where I bought bagels and other exotic foods I had never tasted before and even food I had tasted before, like rice pudding—but there never was a rice pudding like the one you could get at Bassell's Lunch on Yonge Street.

BLACK-EYED SUSANS

Although black-eyed Susans grow almost everywhere, I associate them most with the Cariboo country of British Columbia —dry ochre earth, sagebrush, tumbleweed, pine trees.

Years ago we lived on the damp West Coast, but after we bought our first car, Bruno, Sasha, and I often drove up to Pavilion Lake and discovered that dry, aromatic countryside.

In those days we did a lot of drawing —landscapes, studies of trees —and only admired the black-eyed Susans.

MOIIY LAMB B

A. Y. Jackson and Friends

When I had settled in the CWAC barracks at St. Clair and Avenue Road, I wrote to A. Y. Jackson and asked if I could visit him at his studio and show him my illustrated war diary.

He was a kind fellow. He liked kids; he liked almost everyone, but he and I, we loved each other right from that first meeting. I arrived after supper around twilight. Trees were rustling in the park, and the three-storied studio building was isolated from the noisy city streets. Jackson lived on the second floor and I climbed the oiled stairs to knock at his door. He had a big room with a small balcony at one end; snowshoes were crossed and hanging on the railing. There was an easel, of course, with a canvas on it, the smell of oil paint and turps, magazines and clippings, a kettle on a hot plate, and a wicker chair. Everything slightly soft and dusty in the early evening light. He smoked endless cigarettes from 5 o'clock on, and he cocked his head when he listened to me because he was slightly deaf. He had a clean, hard, eastern Canadian accent.

We talked about my father at first, since that was our connection. After that I went to see A. Y. all the time, often bringing a bottle of Canadian wine. And he looked at my war diary and we talked about Tolstoy's *War and Peace* and all sorts of things. There was a cosy little shack behind the studio building where Tom Thomson used to live. He painted directly on the walls. Once I had supper there with Uncle Alex —as I had begun to call A. Y. —and Keith McIvor, who was a longtime friend of the Group of Seven. I loved the smell of that shack, the smell of a single man's housekeeping.

Uncle Alex also introduced me to Francis Loring and Florence Wilde, two women sculptors quite famous in those days, and to Charles Comfort. We met him at a Chinese restaurant on Elizabeth Street. Comfort was an official Canadian war artist on leave from Europe. He was every inch a captain; everything about him was neat, polished, and shiny and he was friendly and kind. I felt I was among the gods. I wanted very much to be a war artist, too, instead of going to drafting school, but there wasn't much chance then, although much later, when I did become one, I'm sure Jackson had something to do with it.

I had something to do with it too, of course. I never stopped drawing. The CWACs in the bathroom, or the dining hall, or on parade, or something. Once I took some of my work to a Canadian magazine called *New World*, which actually published some of my drawings.

While at the art school in Vancouver, I had seen some of David Milne's work, and I wanted very much to meet him, but no one knew where he was. A man called Douglas Duncan handled Milne's work. Duncan was an aristocrat. He looked like one of the Bloomsbury Group – tall, thin, elegant, bony face, and wavy hair – long for those days. He had a place off Charles Street called the Picture Loan. The day I went to see him, he sat back in his fine chair, smoking a cigarette very slowly, and gently putting the long ashes into a beautiful bubble glass ashtray. I was so enthusiastic I bought a watercolour of Milne's called "Mushrooms and a Maple Leaf" for $35 – two months' and a week's pay for a private in the army. I still have the painting and I still love it, not just because of its subject, but because of the way it's been transposed into the most economical language.

Milne knew what a line did on wet paper and what earth looked like at the end of a mushroom stem. There's no illustration of a mushroom, even no real mushroom, that quite comes up to his. When I see mushrooms in the woods in August I see Milne's mushrooms, just as some people see Turners instead of sunsets.

I asked Douglas Duncan if I could meet Milne, but he said no, I couldn't; he lived quietly in some small Ontario town and only Duncan knew where. After the war when I was married and pregnant, Bruno and I were invited to stay with a woman we hardly knew at a place called Uxbridge. When we arrived she told us she had invited some local artists to tea. She named them for us and added, "I didn't invite a strange artist who lives down the road. He's antisocial. I think his name is Milne."

"Oh," I shrieked, jumping up, "Please don't invite anyone but him!"

She was surprised, but agreed. And Milne came by himself. He looked like a gentle New Englander to me, with a strong, lined face, flannelette shirt, big boots. We talked of mushrooms. He didn't stay long and he asked us not to mention our meeting, but that was long ago and it doesn't matter any more.

I visited Douglas Duncan's quite often while I was stationed in Toronto. I met a strange short man there called Scotty Wilson who drew snakes with clean, short, coloured pencil lines. They were primitive works and at that time Scotty Wilson was fairly well known. Years later, when Bruno and I were living in Streatham, a suburb of London, with our wrestler-artist friend, George Gordienko, I went to buy coffee on the high street at a shop with a roasting machine in the window and brown sacks of every kind of coffee in the world set in rows along the floor.

"You're a Canadian lady, aren't you, love?" the proprietress asked. And when I said I was, she said, "I knew a Canadian gentleman once when we was in the circus together. His name was Scotty Wilson."

I enjoy these overlappings in life.

WILD IRIS

The blue flags are flying in the marsh again. They hate to be picked so I have to take my paints to them.

46

MOLLY LAMB B

I also first met Miller Brittain at Douglas Duncan's. He had a white, strained face and he was wearing an RCAF uniform, a sergeant's, I think. He was on leave after more than forty bombing missions over Germany. He wasn't cut out for it; his nerves were bad. Later he was made a war artist, but I don't think he ever really recovered from that bombing experience. After the war he came to my wedding, although I really met him much later on in New Brunswick.

Miller was a New Brunswicker. He lived and worked in Saint John in the 1930s. There was a small group of painters there who were good comrades and shared a cultural life in that dark, hilly town. Some time after Bruno and I moved to Fredericton, Lady Dunn, Lord Beaverbrook's widow, organized an international art exhibition. It was a gala affair and all the big art fellows were there from all over the world. And Norman Mailer's wife, Lady Jean Campbell who was Lord B's daughter, was there, too. Norman didn't come, though.

The exhibition opened on a cool September evening. The trumpeters from the army band at Camp Gagetown flanked the main doors and blew a fanfare into the crowd. Lady Dunn, slim and dressed in white, threw her arms wide and said, "I declare this exhibition (pause) open."

The gallery was packed. I was there milling about with everyone else, when suddenly I caught sight of Miller, whom I hadn't seen since my wedding. We embraced and he took my hand and guided me through the door to a bench by the river. It was cold and we were suddenly overcome with shyness and didn't know what to say. Finally I told him I had seen a National Film Board film called "Painters of a Province," and thought it was a bad film, but that he had come across very well.

"Gosh, Miller, you haven't changed a bit!" I said.

"Oh, yes I have," he said and he whipped out his false teeth.

We were both tongue-tied again and went back to the crowded gallery. After more years went by I went to visit him in Saint John, where he lived in a huge Georgian house near the water. He was a widower and although many people loved him and respected his work, he was lonely and desolate. He was surrounded by beautiful objects, and the feeling of the place reminded me of that Buenel film, *Veridiana*.

On the third floor was a ballroom which Miller used as a studio, and he let me go there. On an easel was a big canvas, a portrait half-done of the industrialist K. C. Irving. It looked as if Irving was wearing red lipstick. Scattered about the floor were his drawings, fragments of Miller's inner visions. I went downstairs and said good-bye, but just before I left he gave me two silver spoons that had been made in Saint John over a hundred years ago. That was the last time I saw him.

Ottawa

Back to my army days. After my drafting course in Toronto, I was posted to Ottawa. Although I had failed the course, I was expected to make myself useful making detailed drawings of engines, wheel bases, and differentials of army vehicles. It was a farce. I was useless and bored and not too happy at the Glebe barracks where I lived. It was summer 1943, and Ottawa was humid and sweltering. We CWACs had uniforms that wouldn't stay pressed and the brass buttons were sticky and filmy from the wet heat, and our commanding officer was a great one for turning us out on parade every morning. There were only four or five irons among an awful lot of CWACs —three hundred or so. If we were conscientious about the morning inspection (if we weren't, we were CB'd at night) we had to spend our evenings waiting in line to press our uniforms — this after a supper of hot, thick stew and blancmange, and the torrid atmosphere of the mess hall at the hottest part of the day. We were edgy and angry and it was the only time we came close to rioting, and it gave me a good taste of what it must be like to be a civil servant in a meaningless job in Ottawa.

My social life was another story. First, I made friends with a guard named Leo. He was from Prince Edward Island and was what they called a "runner." He was supposed to take important messages from one headquarters to another, but the only time I ever saw him run was at lunchtime when he'd be off to Cartier Square to fry some eggs and chips in the old drill hall. I'd go with him and eat out of sheer boredom. I became fat and sweaty. Fried eggs and chips, and stew in the evening in that incredible heat.

I had time off, though, and often went to the National Gallery where I met the director, Harry McCurry, who knew my father. He and his wife Dorothy were good to me. They had a pleasant house on the Driveway and often had me to dinner, and on weekends they took me to their summer place at Kingsmere in the Gatineau Hills. It was beautiful there.

Goodridge Roberts, the painter, worked up there, but I did not meet him until much later. He was somebody who really felt that countryside, and he captured it in the most unsensational and right way.

RED POPPIES

There is a place in London where we lived for a time called Cleaver Square. It has a pub at one end and the London City and Guilds' Art School at the other, and in between are two and three-storied Georgian row houses which used to be let to working people. In the 1950s, professional people discovered the Square, and avocado, pink, and orange replaced the dark green and black of the doors; inside, chic wallpaper, central heat, bathrooms, and paintings took over from aspidistras and fumed oak.

The gardens changed more than anything else — I know, because we lived between the old and the new. On one side a dear old man and his wife kept their place in perfect order — in front a small garden with a picket fence, and in the back a maze of little paths leading nowhere in particular with a bed of ferns in the middle. But Stephen and Edith on our other side had a House Beautiful garden — a tiny immaculate lawn, white forsythia trailing along the brick wall, and a row of busy lizzies in a border backed by delphiniums and roses. In a corner grew some red poppies — Stephen had brought the seeds back from Greece. He gave us some and now they grow here in Fredericton and seed themselves every year. They, of all flowers, almost paint the watercolours for me.

The Queen Mother gave Stephen and Edith a prize for the best garden in Kennington, but I wonder, would she have had she known that Stephen put his garden debris into the trunks of cars parked in the Square?

50

MOllY LAMB B

Dorothy and Harry McCurry's place was beside Mackenzie King's estate and sometimes in the evenings we wandered about his phony ruins. Once I saw him there walking with his dog. Mackenzie King did actually build ruins. What a curious man! The ruins were rather romantic, though.

That summer I also met Kathleen Fenwick. She invited me to lunch in her apartment after Mr. McCurry had introduced us at the National Gallery. She was then the curator of prints and drawings and looked as though Joyce Grenville could take her off beautifully. She was fair, slim, and toothy, her blonde hair parted in the middle and coiled around her head. She spoke with a very English inflection and wore good suits and expensive Liberty blouses and maybe Clarke shoes. She was a shrewd curator and had amassed a rare and valuable collection of drawings for Canada, but somehow it was always hard to get to see them. They were seldom on the walls.

One would never think to meet Kathleen that she was a strong and clever curator, because she was so vague, always drifting off into little singing monologues like "Angela Thirkell wrote Wild Thrawberrieth." When I first went to her apartment I sat in her beautifully furnished living room, while she, who I'm sure didn't entertain often, sang little songs to herself in the kitchen, "Soup, soup, where are you, you naughty little can of soup? Oh, spoon, there you are." She was a vague driver, too, and she owned a well-preserved Ford with a rumble seat. Sometimes she'd take me out to the McCurrys, generally following Donald Buchanan in his car. There was a great Canadian. I don't know what his job was at that time, something to do with the National Gallery, curator of Canadian art perhaps. He wasn't handsome: short, wispy hair, gnomelike face, and he couldn't hear well. His manner was offhand and brusque and they say he turned off his hearing aid when he was bored.

In the early 1950s he used to come to Vancouver from Ottawa to see the studios of the West Coast painters and select their work for big international biennial shows. That was the flowering time for Alan Jarvis, the flamboyant then new director of the National Gallery. Donald was on his staff and, I suspect, did a lot of the work. But Jarvis got everyone whipped into a lather of excitement.

Bruno and I lived in Lynn Valley then in a little post and beam house that Bruno and Doug Shadbolt designed and which we had built ourselves. And Donald, who'd been visiting painters all day, would arrive around five or six o'clock and I'd feel that he must want to go to the bathroom. All that way from Ottawa, and so on, but when I'd ask him he would have turned off his hearing aid. But he really knew art, and he was probably one of the most discerning art critics we've ever had in this country.

Donald knew art and he knew wine. He had vintner friends in France and took stunning photographs of them. Around 1960 when Bruno and I with Sasha and Anny lived in Cleaver Square in London, we took a two-week journey to Italy. It was April and we were in a beautiful, cheap hotel in Venice, just by the Rialto Bridge. I have never loved a place more. Our hotel lost the spring sun early, so one evening Bruno and I walked to the end of the canal where there was a more opulent hotel with a terrace where we could have a drink in the last light of the setting sun. We had just got settled when a voice behind us shouted, "Bobaks!" It was Donald, who was there arranging an exhibition for the Venice Biennale. It was good to see him. I asked him to stay with us in London on his way home. He seemed pleased, said that he would like that, and did turn up. We went to Battersea Park, he took some photographs of us and little Anny, and we all felt cheerful. But what I enjoyed most of all was that he asked me if I liked washing shirts.

"Oh yes!" I said and so I did because I got a kick out of going to the laundromat which was run by a gaunt Cockney woman called Lil who gave everyone hell if they put their butts in the artificial flower planter or poured too much soap into the machine so that it foamed onto the floor. "Number eight, you're a leakin', lovey," she'd shout, throwing the mop about.

So I washed Donald's shirts. They were a hundred percent cotton, very fine shirts, and when I brought them home I ironed them. He sat in the kitchen watching me and enjoying the peculiar smell that ironing makes. He said it reminded him of home.

During Expo year and long before, he was very busy collecting art for that giant show. The last time I saw him was in his office in one of Montreal's high buildings, probably the Place Ville Marie. He died soon afterwards. One of his hobbies was photography and apparently he'd taken some photos of people in Lower Town Ottawa. One day he decided to deliver the prints to his subjects. By mistake, he left them lying on the roof of his car. As he was driving away, he suddenly remembered them and got out to retrieve them and it was then he was hit by an oncoming car.

Jim Beveridge told us later that Donald's funeral in the Gatineau was magnificent. Everyone was there from all walks of life – the people who'd worked with him, the people he'd photographed, the people who loved him. It was a very cold day with driving sleet, with a fiery Presbyterian minister holding his hand up against the blizzard and commending Donald Buchanan to the earth. I don't know if that's quite how it was, but I believe it anyway.

ANEMONES

Years ago when Bruno and I spent a winter in Cornwall in England, I once saw red and purple anemones growing wild beneath a thorn hedge, and now they always remind me of that winter when we gathered mussels from the rocks on the beach and met Sydney Graham, the poet, at the local pub.

MOLLY LAMB B

The Prize

But back to the 1940s. The army decided it could do without my drawings of the insides of trucks. I was posted to Hamilton, where there was a huge trade school full of "zombies" — men who didn't volunteer to go overseas. There must have been two or three thousand at the trade school and one unit of CWACs. My job was to work in a shop making charts on how to cut meat. There were two good commercial artists there, too. They did a competent job, and my drawings looked like caricatures beside theirs. I couldn't do lettering, either, but I tried and I still have a drawing of myself carrying one of my charts to the cook's school — how to carve lamb.

One day a bulletin came around announcing a painting competition. The prize was a war bond and there would be an exhibition of the work in the National Gallery. I worked away at a little oil of my friends lining up outside the mess hall, and when it was finished, I sent it to Ottawa. When the time came for the judging, I was rejected. It was a stunning blow. I've had lots of rejections since, but none of them as bad as the first one. I must have suffered for a week before I heard that the rejection slip was a mistake and I was accepted after all, and, better than that, I had won second prize.

I was invited to come to receive my war bond from Princess Alice herself. My officer gave me leave, and I packed my kit bag and set out, hitchhiking through the little Ontario towns. When I got there I was dirty and tired and my hair was all over the place. I went to the Chateau, washed my face, and tried to find a hairdresser. It wasn't easy. Everyone I tried was busy. At last I walked into a place on Bank Street — linoleum floor, old permanent wave machines. I knew I should leave but didn't, and what that woman did to me! I came out just before I was due to get my prize from Princess Alice with red hot ears and a head of dried frizz.

In spite of my hair it was a beautiful night, dazzling with uniforms and evening dresses and jewels and even a film crew. Bruno Bobak won first prize and I shared second with a soldier called Robert Bruce. Neither of them was there. Bruno was in Europe.

When I became a war artist and met him in London, he told me he'd seen the film in Holland and wondered who the girl with the frizzy hair was. Winning that prize helped us both get the job we had both wanted for a long time — to be war artists.

I still had to wait almost a year, but I managed to get out of Hamilton and the canteen and join the army show as a set designer.

I worked for Art Price who later became a sculptor, but at that time he was responsible for the scenery and the lighting of these little shows. Captain Romney Brent, a British actor, and a little dark woman from New York called Felicia Sorrell were the two I remember best. They were so sophisticated! They'd get all the girls in a line and get them tap dancing and singing and doing specialty numbers. Bob Farnham was the music conductor. I thought everyone was great.

Wayne and Shuster came back from Europe one day and I remember talking about Cezanne – still my favourite painter – to Johnny Wayne.

My officer was Ed Harris and he and his wife Ruth became my very dear friends. Ed's sister even gave me a Schiaparelli dress! Best of all, Ed encouraged me to paint in my spare time and the National Gallery agreed to supply me with paints and canvasses. I remember going to Loomis and Toles and buying yellows and reds and greens and blues and ochres. There's nothing like a tube of paint – better than cosmetics any day! So I painted canvasses and made sets and had a terrific time. I lived on what they then called "subsistence," which meant I didn't have to be in barracks. I had a place on Prince Arthur Street with a family called Andison. Mr. Andison was a professor of French at the University of Toronto and his wife Maybelle translated the works of Jacques Maritain, the French philosopher, into English. They were extraordinarily kind to me. I used to come home from work with a compressed cube of pea soup which I thought would be fine for my supper, but Maybelle always insisted I sit down at the table with them. Gordon would fuss about the salad dressing, crushing garlic with a wooden pestle in a mortar and overseeing everything like a chef.

They allowed me to invite friends over in the evening, and Varley came once or twice. I used to see him wandering down Yonge Street sometimes, lonely and having a rough time, and I think he enjoyed coming to the Andisons for a drink or two.

Leonard Brooks, then a war artist in the navy, also came, and he and Gordon played duets together – Gordon on the piano and Leonard on his violin. And Alberto Garrerro, Glenn Gould's teacher, was a friend of the Andisons and I met him too. How I grew up, how powerful I began to feel, and confident, too! I had never felt easy in even the most ordinary situations, but living with the Andisons made me feel sure and positive.

One day a group of army show performers wanted me to join them for a drink in a pub; something new for me. I was very quiet until I had downed my first drink, then I became the life of the party – at least I felt I was. I ended up in a cathouse near King Street with a fellow who didn't do anything but wet the bed.

I walked home to the Andisons early in the morning. Maybelle looked very wise and very hurt.

"Molly, dear, you're beginning to look coarse," she said.

So much for my emancipation.

FLOWERS FROM CANMORE

In late September one year I went to the Banff School of Fine Arts to teach drawing and painting. I arrived in the middle of the night and fell into bed exhausted. In the morning when I woke up I looked out across the valley to a vast rim of great white mountains and felt I was in Thomas Mann's Magic Mountain, isolated from the world below and breathing only heady air.

I turned on the life there as if nothing else existed. Working, wandering in the woods, eating —the intensity of the experience was new.

The last time I taught in Banff was in the spring when the mountain flowers were out, and one Saturday we went to Canmore —an old western mining town not far from Banff. Iceland poppies grew in front of some of the frame houses and in the meadows outside the town we found shooting stars and something called three-flowered avens —someone said they were "sleepyheads" because they look as if about to burst into bloom but never do. And there were wild strawberry flowers, hairy violet crocus, and Indian paintbrush.

One is not supposed to pick wild flowers in Banff but it's all right in Canmore, so I gathered a bouquet, brought it back to my room, and painted it over and over again until the flowers withered.

58

MOlly LAMB B

Europe

I went from the army show to officers' training at St. Anne de Bellevue because, finally, in 1945 when the war was almost over, I had made it with the war artist business.

Learning to be an officer was easy and amusing. The National Gallery bought my paintings at the army show, and they sent me a five-hundred dollar cheque. I'd never seen so much money in my life – the cadets and I spent a lot of it in the town one evening.

The last day of our training we had a parade and inspection. A general from MD2 took the salute. We had white tabs over our one pip, second lieutenant, and we all marched about briskly before lining up for the inspection. The general stopped to talk to every fifth or sixth girl, and when he got to me, he said tiredly, "Where are you from?"

"Galiano Island, sir," I answered smartly.

We marched around again. This time he stood in the middle as we approached one by one to have our tabs cut and our pips exposed. When my turn came I stood before him and heard him say, "Where are you from?"

"Galiano Island," I answered.

"There's an awful lot of you from there, aren't there?" he said.

On VE Day I hitchhiked to Toronto, joining the jubilant crowds in Napanee and other towns along the way.

Before I went overseas I was sent to the historical section headquarters in Ottawa to wait for my boat and to become familiar with the war art program. There I met Ed Hughes. To my mind he was the best war artist. He had gone to the Vancouver School of Art and was a great draftsman and a skilled painter. But, much more than that, he is one of those artists I call private – he has found a unique and personal way of painting, outside the current fashions and movements. When I first met him he had not found his personal style; the work he had done in Europe for the army was meticulous and illustrative. He had been sent home, probably feeling he had failed. Later he was posted to the Aleutian Islands off the West Coast, and there he did the great canvasses of snow and troops with all their insignia and detail that I think are so fine.

But while in Ottawa in that old building on Napean Street, he barricaded himself behind piled up filing cabinets and I felt it was a privilege to be allowed to see his work and talk to him. I'd knock on the filing cabinets and he'd shift a few of them to let me in. He had pale, pale blue eyes and he was shy, but he knew my enthusiasm for his work was genuine.

In early June of 1946 I was sent to Kitchener where the last contingent of CWACs was being organized to leave for overseas. We took a troop train to Halifax and boarded the *Ile de France* for landing somewhere near Glasgow. I guess I needed Maybelle Andison's motherly advice again, because I met two fellows on the boat and decided to stay in Glasgow with them for the evening. After all, I was an officer and could do as I pleased. Well, the boys had to report to a naval air base in Grenoch and never did get back to Glasgow to see me. So I got on a late train to London by myself. At Crewe I was met by army police; by the time I got to Aldershot I found myself in trouble. Luckily it was just a reprimand, so it didn't matter too much.

Aldershot was tense. The Canadian soldiers, overseas for so long, were frustrated and longed to go home. At night they broke windows in the town and otherwise behaved badly. Once going to my post in London by train, I could feel the tenseness in our compartment. We were three CWAC officers, an army chaplain, and some male privates. The privates made suggestive remarks, and one CWAC captain pulled her rank on them; then the privates got quite ugly and frightening. So the chaplain started talking about hockey – it didn't work, though.

The army war artists had their headquarters in Holborne across from Chancery Lane in a building called Fairfax House. There I met Will Ogilvie and Alex Colville and Campbell Tinning and Bruno Bobak (who had won first prize in the army art competition) and Tom MacDonald and Lawren Harris, Jr.

Alex Colville was a dedicated, meticulous person. He took his work seriously and painted with precision and concern for detail, and when I think of it now, it's easy to see the logical way his work developed. I remember his war paintings as thoughtful and observant, almost ground works of what was to come later – the canvasses even then had that arrested time feeling.

One day Alex, Bruno, and I went to Kingston on Thames together and hired a punt. We always did the pleasant, sane things with Alex, but generally in the evening, a lot of the war artists, me included, went to Short's Pub in Chancery Lane and caroused.

I had a wonderful time in London being flighty and free. And painting, yes, I did that too.

After three months in England I was sent to Holland, to a place called Appeldoorn. I flew for the first time in my life. We all sat around the sides of the plane and were issued paper bags in case we got sick. I kept craning my head around to look out the window to see what the earth looked like. I remember the sea shimmering in a silver arc below me.

NASTURTIUMS

One April I went to Boston with Bruno and we visited a vast Venetian palace there, which a lady called Mrs. Gardiner had had brought over from Italy, brick by brick and tile by tile. She had it filled with paintings and sculptures and furniture — all of which I have forgotten, but I remember the great glass-covered inner courtyard, where from the upper balcony trailed long magnificent strands of nasturtiums.

Ever since that visit we have grown nasturtiums too — all summer they sprawl from urns on each side of our front steps, and in the winter Bruno brings them inside, where they crawl up and down the front windows flattening their pad-like leaves against the panes and sending out vermilion and yellow flowers in between a profusion of green leaves.

MOLLY LAMB B

It was mellow early fall weather in Holland. I was billeted with a tiny woman called Miss Meister. She had a tiny kettle, a tiny house, everything tiny and tidy. I felt so big and well fed I often brought her raisins and butter from the CWAC mess, which made her cry with delight. She hadn't seen such things for five years.

"Moj," she used to cry, "Moj!" and wring her hands.

I had an army car called a Hup given to me and a driver who had been through the Italian campaign and who was hostile to me at first, which I understood. He didn't want to drive a CWAC second lieutenant fresh from Canada all over the place. Eventually we became friends and I gave him cognac from the mess.

One night I wanted to go to Baarn to see a Canadian theatre troupe who called themselves "The Tin Hats" and were modelled on the Dumbells of World War I fame. But my driver had got into the brandy, and as we sped down a wet, dark road lined with big trees he lost control; we skidded into one of the trees and were thrown on to the highway. Sparks flashed from the engine, and before we knew it some figures rushed out of the darkness out of the woods and started to loot the Hup. I'd put some cognac in there for The Tin Hats, too. We didn't try to stop them; we were far too shocked. Eventually we discovered we were just shaken and bruised, so we waited until another army truck came along, flagged it down, and went back to Appeldoorn.

I had to do some explaining, but we soon got another Hup and were on our way again.

I did a lot of drawing in Germany, Belgium, Holland, and even got to Paris, which at that time was grim. It was a strange time to be in Europe; the war was just over and everyone was exhausted, frustrated, and poor. The Dutch were totally fed up with foreign troops, even Canadian. Maybe Canadians more than anyone, though we were regarded as their liberators. There was much black marketing and violence. Every day you'd read about some body being fished out of a canal.

One night in Brussels I met two UNRRA men who boastfully showed me three lorries full of new American tires they were selling for a small fortune. The old values did not seem to make sense any more, except to take what you could before you went back to teaching school or working in an office, and the Europeans just wanted to pick up what they could of their lives and be left alone.

One night I saw the navy show – a huge success wherever it played. It was a command performance in Amsterdam, in a big, ornate theatre with a top brass audience. During the performance most of the cast were drunk and made impromptu swings from the curtains and threw buckets of water all over the stage. It was a shambles, and it summed up the mood of the times.

Marriage

Late in 1945 I went back to London and we were all sent home. Bruno went first. He and I had decided we'd get married when I got back to Canada. He came to Ottawa to meet my troop train and we went on to his parents' house on Ossington Avenue in Toronto. Dzicdzik, his father, had strung out a huge sign – right across Ossington Avenue – "Welcome home, Bruno and Molly" in great red letters. I had laryngitis and when I went into the house to meet him and Bruno's mother, Babi, I couldn't make a sound.

"Hey Bruno!" said Dzicdzik, "Can she talk?" My voice came back and he was reassured.

He and Babi set about preparing a real Polish wedding for us. Babi made mountains of pierogi, cabbage rolls, honey cake, polish sausages, sour cream, sauerkraut, and stuffed peppers, and Dzicdzik looked after the schnapps.

We were married in the Church of All Nations – the name seemed right. Maybelle Andison stood beside me and Aba Bayefsky, a war artist in the air force, stood beside Bruno.

That night we had a big banquet at the Polish Organization hall. A.Y. Jackson made a speech. He and the Andisons were at the head table together with us, as well as the leaders of the Organization. Bruno and I were presented with a set of Rogers Brothers First Love flatware, the service for eight, which I still use. We danced like mad and had a grand party all night long.

After that the fun was over for a time. Most of the war artists went back to Ottawa to finish their paintings, as did Bruno and I. It was hard to find a place to live, but finally a kind woman who used to scrub the floors in the Parliament Buildings, a Mrs. Greenberg, rented us a bedroom in her house in Lower Town. It was dreary and yellowish and we cooked on a one-plate electric burner perched on an orange crate. We didn't think much of marriage. Soon I became pregnant and got sick every morning. I'd have to rush to the bathroom, where I'd meet Mrs. Greenberg's daughter about to leave for work.

"I'd sure love to get married," she'd say, "How'd you get a fella?"

I felt like telling her, "Don't try Jenny, don't try. Just be content as you are."

In the spring of 1946 the National Gallery planned a big exhibition of war art, to be

TANSIES

The best tansies I know grow beside the CPR tracks outside Montreal. If you live in Fredericton and take the train to Montreal, you first have to take a bus from the old CPR station on York Street to get to Fredericton Junction, twenty-two miles away. It's great fun, especially in winter when the hoary train lumbers in from Saint John around ten o'clock at night —icicles hanging from its Cyclops eye, heavy sighs of steam rising in the cold air. Or, in late spring while you wait on the platform and the twilight sky is faintly red and you can hear the frogs yodelling beside the Oromocto River. In the old days, so they say, the meat, milk, butter, and vegetables used to come aboard at the Junction from a farm that still stands on the hill, but now they serve canned beans and Salisbury steak. Still, I love to take the train and ride all night through Maine and arrive around dawn. It's in August that you can see the lush saffron-coloured tansies that make you want to jump off and gather armfuls of them and smell their powerful medicinal smell.

66

MOLLY LAMB B

opened by Lord Alexander. All the war artists were to be there and a great crowd of illustrious people from the army, Church, embassies, and government were invited. I could hardly button up my uniform – the only pregnant war artist, I imagine, Canada has ever had.

Some of the other war artists were rather drunk. One had a little trickle of Sen Sen running down his chin. Sen Sen was the Clorets of the 1940s. Another had mud all over his uniform, someone else had lost his Sam Browne, and yet another had fallen down the gallery stairs, but somehow we managed to line up to receive congratulations from Lord Alexander.

Bruno and I went back to Toronto with the idea that maybe he'd make frames for a living. A.Y. Jackson was away painting in the West and let us live in his studio. My stomach was getting bigger, and I worried how I'd ever get out of his building if there happened to be a fire. Jackson had a rope tied to the floor of his little bedroom that was the only escape. But I didn't dwell on the possibility much.

We had lots of visitors: George and Kay Pepper who lived in another studio, Charles Comfort, Tom Wood, who'd been a navy war artist and offered Bruno a job in the Exhibition Commission in Ottawa. That was the department that used to exhibit wheat sheaves and bottled fruit and lumps of coal. But they were getting much more slick in their display work.

Bruno went to Ottawa and I stayed behind to wait for the baby.

Early in October my mother came with Kathleen Shackleton, her old friend, whom she had first met in Montreal in her laundry days when Kathleen worked for a newspaper. Later Kathleen did pastel portraits for the CPR, and Dad photographed her in a fur parka. She was a strong, independent woman with a great Irish warmth. Often she was penniless, and when she lived in the Ritz in Vancouver, she had once phoned Mum and asked her if she would buy a brass bed for twelve dollars. When Mum agreed to buy it, Kathleen said, "Good, now I can ask you to dinner and we shall finish it off with a good brandy."

When she visited me in A.Y.'s studio I was often restless, wondering if I was about to give birth, and she would say, "Not tonight, my dear, not tonight. The moon isn't right."

Finally when the moon was right and I went to a nearby hospital to have Sasha, she rode all the way up to the top of Yonge Street on the streetcar to pick me some wild flowers.

In Ottawa Mum had found us a cottage, three of them, in fact, in a row, out in Hog's Back, with the impossible addresses of number one, two, and three Cosy Lane, a pump out front, and three backhouses behind. We lived in one, had the second as a studio, and rented the third.

Going Home

Eventually, like so many other homesick Westerners, I lured Bruno to Galiano Island, saying we could live on fish and would only have to buy sugar, tea, and coffee. Of course, that wasn't the case. Bruno built us a small wooden cottage on my mother's new property at Retreat Cove at the north end of the island. She had rented out the cove to a fly-by-night sawmill run by a sweet but ineffectual man named Stan, who in the process of going bankrupt, made a terrible shambles of the land. He begged Mum to feed his grumbling crew of nine men, as he had no money to hire a cook or pay salaries.

Mum turned her big barn into a cookhouse and I became the bull cook. Life was an endless round of huge meals. What a stupid, terrible time it was! We had a big wood stove, and once we bought a whole cow and Mum and I cut it up. What the men couldn't eat, we bottled. The sweet smell of the endless bones and the soup and the stews became nauseating. Furthermore, Stan could not pay us.

Before long Bruno and I were forced to think of ourselves, and so it was decided he should go to Vancouver and find a job. He got one at the Vancouver School of Art teaching design. Our great friend Ron Thom, who I had met at the School before joining the army, told Bruno about some fine cheap lots on Peter's Road in Lynn Valley. He had already bought two or three himself and was beginning to build a house of his own design there. So Bruno bought two lots right beside Ron's. Meanwhile at Retreat Cove, I went down to the wharf with a bucket of red paint and marked BB on the ends of a stack of lumber—my pay for bull cooking for Stan's men. And then I got a tug and a barge and had the lumber towed to North Vancouver. Eventually we built out first real house with it.

While we were building we lived in the West End in a rooming house in a small ugly room. At night we would put a blanket over Sasha's crib so he could go to sleep in the dark.

Vancouver was changing. For one thing, community centres were being organized because so many mothers had to work. Near us was a place called Gordon House. They had rooms where retired people could play cards and I once painted a mural there, but they didn't like it. They also had an all-day play school for the children of the district. I

PINK CINERARIA

Fredericton has a farmers' market as most cities and towns do. Once it used to be just a market, but now it's almost a statement against supermarkets and plastic packaging. Its character has changed slightly, and among the stalls of eggs and meat and homemade bread and fish, young craftsmen sell pots and lamps and wooden toys and jewellery. It's a place of gentle protest, a place where one can get a sense of the simple life which is gone. Maybe it's only a pretend place but I love it and I go there most Saturday mornings to buy liver and smoked pigs' jowls and cracked eggs and cinerarias.

Cinerarias are a luxury in this hard, late-starting land, but in Vancouver they cost very little and sit in rows outside the small grocery stores. When Anny was ill with scarlet fever I brought this pink cineraria to her apartment, bought watercolour paper and paints from my old friend Al Maxwell, and painted it.

MOLLY LAMB B

used to take Sasha to English Bay every day, but often it was raining and you could only feed so many birds and make so many sand castles. When I heard about Gordon House I went there and asked them if they would take Sasha. He was talking by this time and was by nature an independent little boy. They allowed him to come, although he wasn't quite two, on the condition that he be happy.

And so one morning I took him there. When I left I didn't dare look back; I was afraid he was staring at me from the window, feeling abandoned and betrayed. Luckily he soon came to love Gordon House and I was able to go up to Lynn Valley and work on the house. Ron Thom, who first thought he would be a painter, had become passionate about architecture and was a disciple of Frank Lloyd Wright. He not only designed his own house, but he'd confront everyone who bought lots on Peter's Road and begged them to let him design their houses also – for nothing, of course. Bruno, together with another young architect, Doug Shadbolt, designed ours – a simple post and beam structure with a high shed roof. We all worked furiously whenever we could. I didn't do any measuring, but I was a strong labourer.

Some mornings we would arrive to find Ron in the middle of his unfinished living room next door, fast asleep in a canvas chair, having worked the whole night long.

The day came when we all moved in. The houses were liveable, the good trees – cedar and spruce – were left standing, and the slash was burnt. Peter's Road smelled of fir and salal and cedar and wood smoke.

Vancouver

At last Bruno and I had a studio, and we began to paint again. Bruno turned to the British Columbia wild growth—things like water hemlock and the reeds by the sea's rim. His style started to change with his feeling for the weeds and the grasses. Later he found his subjects beyond the Coast range in the high dry hills around Ashcroft and Lilloet. That was when we bought our first car, a second-hand Austin Devon.

Ron Thom apprenticed himself to an architectural firm and designed the British Columbia Electric Building. The early 1950s saw a vital, natural kind of explosion in the city. We artists began to sell our work, and the Vancouver Art Gallery had demonstration nights which were crammed with people. That's when Donald Buchanan and Alan Jarvis paid us visits from Ottawa. And Gordon Smith, our gentle painter friend, won the big prize at the National Gallery. And Arthur Ericson who had been influenced by Gordon Webber, that super teacher for so many young student architects at McGill, was beginning his career.

I must say something about Gordon Webber. First of all, physically he was deformed. His little body seemed crushed and he had a wooden leg. But he designed his own clothes which were quite marvellous and inventive. And his head—ah, that's what one looked at—a halo of blond hair, a young eager face full of wit and passion, darting eyes taking in the world, flushed cheeks, mobile mouth, and a brain which awed his students. He was the catalyst behind much of what had happened in the arts in Canada in the post-war explosion.

Gordon stayed with us once when we lived in numbers one, two, and three Cosy Lane in Hog's Back. I put him in number two. When I brought him his morning tea, he was hiding under the bedcovers, but a complete replica of himself—his hat, ascot, silk shirt, and wooden leg—were hanging from a peg on the wall.

He was doing a big international display for the Exhibition Commission at that time; that's how we met him. It was a huge project which he designed, using lots of electrical effects, very advanced techniques. And I remember hearing that at the grand opening the Minister of External Affairs or Trade and Commerce, or whoever he was, pushed the

SIMPLE SUMMER FLOWERS

Fredericton is the only place I know where I can walk from my house to the Air Canada office in bare feet. That's because there is still grass all along the river bank although "they" are threatening to put in a four-lane highway. Down the bank grow daisies and wild campanulas and I never come home from town without picking a few. The poppies are from our garden —so far they do not grow wild here —but next spring maybe I'll sprinkle some seeds about and take a few to a lake near the Royal Road to scatter on the grave of Anny's old horse, Missy.

74

MOLLY LAMB B

button to make the display twinkle and flash and do other extraordinary things, there was a short circuit and the exhibition plunged into darkness.

I, too, did a mural for the Exhibition Commission. It was for a trade fair in Australia and I used to take the baby to work with me. I'd paint on a ladder and climb down when it was time to feed him. The mural wasn't appreciated, though, because as usual I had not done any research. I had painted hockey players racing around the ice with field hockey sticks!

But the 1950s were growing, exuberant times for us and our painter friends – Don Jarvis, Bruce and Joan Boyd, Gordon Smith, Alistair Bell, and our architect friends who were making their West Coast indoor-outdoor houses. Life became positive and less of a struggle.

At this time A.Y. Jackson paid a visit to Vancouver, and stayed with his old friend, Lawren Harris, who lived on Belmont Avenue in the University area. Harris's wife Bess was away and the two old friends had a fine time together. They were both to give lectures at the Vancouver Art Gallery and I was invited to introduce A.Y. because everyone knew I loved him. Jackson spoke simply, about eating Roman Meal in Algonquin Park when the Group of Seven were working up there together. Harris, far more intellectual and articulate, spoke of ideas and philosophies. We invited them to dinner and the Bells came too. I was a margarine cook in those days, but we were all so excited and the two old friends arrived feeling so mellow, that the meal wasn't important. What was important was something I had arranged earlier – a visit to Varley's studio up by the water shed in Lynn Valley. His wife Maude was still living there. I knew, because one day she came to my door selling Avon cosmetics. I recognized her because she looked so like Mr. Varley. Before the dinner I went to see her and asked if I might bring Harris and Jackson, and she said, "That would be fine."

That's what we did. We all went up to the studio.

"Hello Lawren, hello Alex," she said, as she opened the door.

"Hello, Maude," they said. It must have been years since they met. Jackson had never approved of Fred Varley's bohemianism and felt sympathy for Maude, although she didn't need it. She held no malice or bitterness against her husband. She took our coats and we came into the room.

It smelled of cedar like all old B.C. houses, and it was sparsely furnished and neat.

"Molly, pour the wine, please," said Maude. She had set out a decanter of small homemade white wine and eight or so little Kraft cheese glasses. We sat down and listened to Maude and Alex and Lawren reminisce. Before we left Maude pulled out a black trunk and showed us some early Tom Thomsons and some Varleys. The Thomsons were tonal and smooth – grey seascapes done before he came into his own flood of painting, and I felt we were in on a bit of history that night.

So there we were, working away and slowly getting recognition, but there was another painter in New Westminster called Joe Plaskett who would visit us from time to time, but who had gone on a totally different path. Harris had always thought a lot of Joe —I think Harris had got him an Emily Carr scholarship when Joe went to New York to study with the famous Hans Hoffman, who was the daddy of all the abstract expressionists in the fifties and sixties.

We have one of Joe's paintings from this time. It looks like a blue and red spaceship or something. We should hang it with the others—the ones he painted when he found his personal style.

Joe never became a part of that loose West Coast group. His life had and has a style all its own. He's a brilliant painter whose home is enough of a theme to start him on a series of canvasses about himself and his friends, about the table after a feast, careless white cups, wine glasses, plates, flowers, just as they were when the guests got up from the table. Today he lives in Paris in an ancient house on the Rue Pecquay and I don't believe the Establishment really thinks of him as a Canadian artist. No one can put Joe into a slot.

When he comes home to Canada he has exhibitions from coast to coast. Sometimes he stays with us in Fredericton, and if it's springtime we pick trout lilies in the woods.

We've stayed with him in Paris too. His place is always full of visitors. The last time we were there we met the head of the gay lib of Italy, a Canadian diplomat, an English soprano who sang Mozart at breakfast, and painters, writers, students, a dancer at the Moulin Rouge. I sometimes wonder how Joe ever gets any work done, but he does and he writes me letters telling me of new ideas and themes he's busy with.

CANADA LILY

Here in New Brunswick Canada lilies grow beside rivers and streams and railway tracks. They are for me the finest lily of all — tall, straight stalks branching out at the node like fireworks ending in orange explosions.

They like cold winters, I think, because they don't grow wild in southern Ontario. I once sent some seeds to a friend and she planted them on her farm a little north of Toronto. One did come up, so perhaps we have started something.

78

MOLLY LAMB B

England

During the good times in the 1950s Bruno and I both got fellowships. He got his first, just when Anny was born in 1957. We took her across Canada in a wicker basket on the CPR train and on a Cunard boat from Montreal to Southampton. We settled in Cornwall in a little village called Lelant. It was a shiny green place; luminous, as if everything reflected back from the intensity of the sea. Bruno roamed the moors and grappled with a change in his thinking, and, therefore, a change in his painting. I drew Brussels sprouts in our backyard and sometimes I'd wheel Anny down to the station and ride the toy train to St. Ives all along the rim of the green cliffs. She'd suck away on a bottle of National Health orange juice while I painstakingly drew St. Ives. It was a beautiful time and we met some English painters – Brian Winter, Patrick Heron, Barbara Hepworth, Peter Lanyon, and Karl Weshkey, a German who lived in D.H. Lawrence's old cottage. And we met the poet W. S. Graham – Willy, who was an awful drinker but a sweet man. His poems were all dark and Celtic and washed with the sea.

The St. Ives community was curious – the richer painters seemed to look after the poorer ones. Lanyon and his wife were particularly generous. They lived with their five children in a large, comfortable house on the cliff near the sea, and once when we went to a party there, all the artists were spruced up and wearing their best clothes, but the retired amateur painters were dressed in seamen's jerseys and berets.

Almost all the serious painters in St. Ives were influenced by the New York School, which I thought was sad. They lacked the vitality of the Americans, except Peter Lanyon who could draw like a master and whose big, green, washed abstracts reflected his own experience. Later he died in a glider accident.

The time in Cornwall changed Bruno. He could not face teaching again, nor even the good life in Vancouver. He began painting in oil; until then he had used gouache. He started misty, wet, open canvasses of beaches and moors and Gurney's Head, a craggy promontory on the coast. And when we came home he went up to the top of Ron Thom's B. C. Electric Building and painted Vancouver. Then he went up to Dad's and Vera's house on Capital Hill, high in the east of the city, and made a big canvas from there. He was away and moving, but I was still doing what I'd always done, at least not conscious of any major change in my attitude.

Paris

In 1960 Air France asked me to be a teacher on a tour they were organizing to Paris—fourteen glorious days on the banks of the Seine for only a thousand dollars. I had a Canada Council grant that year and it seemed a good idea to take up Air France's offer — a free flight for myself and Sasha and our lodging at a picturesque but well-equipped hotel on the Left Bank. Twenty-five women signed up. I knew many of them from my teaching days at the Vancouver School of Art and we all loved each other, so it should have been a fine holiday. It wasn't.

First, I almost missed the plane. From then on many plans went wrong – trouble with customs, no plane for us in New York, worse confusion when we got to Paris. We had a disgruntled guide called Yvonne who hated us on sight –she had seen too many like us, I suppose. Every day she was supposed to arrange for a bus to take us around the city, but it always came late and couldn't park, so Yvonne would burst into our disagreeable hotel, where we'd been sitting for hours, and scream, "My group, my group, you must 'urry!"

All the ladies would grab their easels and paints and rush down the narrow street towards the bus and I'd ask the driver to take us to the Place de la Concorde, or the first name that came into my head. Once there, I'd shout my lecture above the traffic noise, and they would settle down and paint the total confusion of Paris traffic.

We did have a few good times. Once when it was raining I took them to visit Isadora Duncan's brother Raymond – somewhere near the Rue de Seine. It wasn't much of a place but at least Raymond was interesting. He was dressed in a white toga and wore a headband around his fringed Dutch cut. He had one or two disciples who were in the same outfit. He loved to talk endlessly, especially to North Americans –he was from the States originally. He invited us to come back that evening as he had arranged a concert. The greatest interpreter of Chopin in the world was going to play.

Some of us did go back after dinner and Raymond led us into a dark back room hung with Persian carpets. There was a small stage and a grand piano. I sat by Raymond who smelled sweet and old, and soon there appeared a big woman leading a small, smiling man towards the stage. He had a pink face surrounded by long silky white hair, wore tails and a shirt with lace flounces at the neck and wrists. The big woman seated him at the piano and he composed himself, winked knowingly at the audience, and began to play.

PEONIES

For a long time painting peonies seemed impossible. There were just too many washable oils in art shops depicting these exotic, smooth flowers in a highlighted smooth bowl, set on a highlighted smooth mahogany table. But why not paint them as if for the first time, in Nan and Ellen's garden here in Fredericton?

MOLLY LAMB B

I don't know if it was Chopin but it certainly sounded like it, and he played on and on, every so often winking and nodding and inviting us by his signal to keep alert for the beautiful passage about to come. When it was over he was led out by the strong woman, bobbing very hard as he went out the door.

Much later I saw the film about Isadora Duncan. At one point in her career she had an accompanist who also was one of her many lovers. I want to believe that this little old fellow was the one.

Because of small adventures like this, and also visits to my friend Joe Plaskett who gave the ladies tea and black olives in his elegant studio, and then let them look at his pastels (and buy them), the fourteen glorious days along the Seine didn't turn out so badly.

When they were over, Bruno brought little Anny to Paris. Joe drove Sasha and me to the Orly airport to meet them. When the door of the big plane swung open we saw a stewardess trying to take Anny's hand to bring her down the steps, but she was furious and flayed her arms in the air. She was followed by Bruno, looking fatigued and resigned. So began the year of my Canada Council fellowship.

We drove through Europe to Norway, sleeping in our French stationwagon and cooking on a propane burner. Norway is another story, and I shan't write it now. I only mention it because it was while we were in Oslo that Bruno received an invitation to become artist-in-residence at the University of New Brunswick. He accepted. The appointment was for one year, and in the fall we left Oslo on a late flight to Iceland and Gander. We flew in an American prop plane through the black blue starry sky and looked down on the blue green icebergs. No lights on the aircraft. It was like a silent, moving dream. And we saw the first Sputnik, too, slowly moving in the opposite direction.

Fredericton, N.B.

In Gander, after we got through the customs, we were confronted with a reproduction of Varley's portrait of Vera. We waited for five hours for a plane to take us to Moncton. When we arrived we were tired and cross. The airport had plastic chairs with the stuffing coming out, and outside a hot September wind blew over a field of dying goldenrod. We had another five-hour wait for the plane to Fredericton, so we decided to hire a car and get there on our own.

I remember thinking, "Why did Mum think this place so beautiful? It's nothing, just small and ugly and poor."

When we got to Fredericton, Bruno asked me to phone Murray Kinloch, the professor we were supposed to contact, and ask him where we were. So I did.

"Hello, is that Professor Kinloch? This is Molly Bobak. Yes, we've just arrived by car from Moncton, and could you tell us how to get to the centre of town?"

"Where are you now?" the Professor asked.

"Well," I said looking out of the phone booth, "There's a store called Neil's Sporting Goods across from here."

"You are in the centre of town," he replied.

The mighty Westerner in me sneered.

That night we could not see the beautiful elm trees, the green river bank, the huge, elegant, wooden houses.

We did notice, though, the spire of Wilmot United Church poking through the green umbrella of the elms. On top was a great hand—one finger pointing to heaven. It's gone now, though; the spire is decaying, and they can't raise the money to restore it. A couple of years ago when I was on the design advisory committee of the post office and we had to find a stamp for the United Church, I tried very hard to convince the committee to use the great hand. But they felt that, in these days, a pointing finger might be misconstrued.

The people at the University had rented the top part of a house on Lansdowne Street for us. When we got there, after being fed by the kind Kinlochs, our hearts sank. It was supposed to be furnished, but when I saw the old chrome table, the plastic

JULY FLOWERS FROM THE HILL

Even in Fredericton progress encroaches on my favourite haunts. There's a hill which is owned by the University of New Brunswick where in winter we used to ski, where in summer were pockets of fat fiddleheads, in June strawberries, in July raspberries, and in autumn wild grapes and blackberries, and, always, flowers. Now some busy person has turned the hill into a Participaction course. The natural trails have been gravelled and every so often there is a trapeze to swing on, a series of posts to leap over, or a log pile to climb. I resist and resent such conscious efforts to keep fit. Why not climb over a fallen log or bend down to pick flowers —columbines, daisies, and lupins?

86

MOLLY LAMB B

curtains with great red roses on yellow plastic, the dirty old refrigerator, and the iron beds with only mattresses on them, I wanted to turn around and run. But we were so tired, we unpacked our sleeping bags and just fell asleep.

The next morning was the day after Labour Day. We walked along the river bank and tried to get some breakfast, but no one had any food because of the long holiday. We ended up in the Metropolitan store, sharing their two last pancakes. We also bought a cheap set of willow-patterned cups and saucers and plates and bowls and some food. I remember being shocked at the prices and the lack of variety – nothing but Kraft cheese.

We bought a mop and a broom, opened the windows, and shook the horrible, ugly mats, then walked up the hill to the campus of the University of New Brunswick and met the president, Colin McKay. Also John Corey, who was in charge of the old army hut art centre. Gradually we began to feel more hopeful.

The early fall weather was mellow and clear. The maples were turning scarlet; the butternut trees were violet, smudging into opaque yellows; towheaded meadows and fields surrounded Fredericton, and the blue Saint John River flowed through the town.

John Corey showed us how to look at life here and later he showed us how to love the winter too. He'd take us into the country in his old car and throw a bear rug or maybe a buffalo robe on to the snow, and we'd have a picnic under the pure blue sky.

He knew everything about New Brunswick. He took us to his old house in Havelock and cooked blueberry muffins for breakfast on his big wood stove, and in summer he'd take us to a brook and cover himself with mud and jump into the clear water and we would do the same thing. That year we learned all about the good wild things like mushrooms, chanterelles and boletus, and high-bush cranberries and apples and fish, and so many things the supermarkets don't supply.

A friend called Herbie Webber, who ran Herbie's Music Store on Queen Street, often brought us rye bread and pastrami and dills from Montreal. He was an enthusiastic collector and had a few small paintings of Jackson's. He loved music and played the violin in a trio. He told me he had once played at the hotel during a lunch for the Queen on one of her visits. He even had the napkin she had used.

Lord Beaverbrook was still alive then and came every year from England to stay in his suite in the Beaverbrook Art Gallery. He was like a king. Even the Fredericton newspaper was run by one of his ex-Fleet Street men, a Brigadier Wardell. It amazed me how much power Lord Beaverbrook had in Fredericton. I remember one day going down Charlotte Street to do a drawing and coming home along the green, past the Beaverbrook Gallery. The old man was sunning himself outside and talking to Colin McKay. He had a soft red slipper on his gouty foot and he looked like an old frog squinting in the sun.

I met him once inside the Gallery. Edwy Cooke, then the curator, had brought an exhibition of contemporary Canadian work to the Gallery. I was teaching an extension class at the University (I started working almost immediately after we arrived in

Fredericton), and was taking my class to see the show. Just as we were coming up from the basement gallery where the show was hung, I met Lord Beaverbrook at the top of the stairs. Edwy introduced me and Lord Beaverbrook said, "What are you showing your students the Canadian for? Aren't my English paintings good enough for you?"

I don't remember my lame reply, but, as a matter of fact, the English collection was terrific—Gainsborough, Sickert, Graham Sutherland, Turner, and others too. Somebody had chosen wisely but I don't think it was he. I once saw a portrait of Christ he had picked up in Jamaica—because the eyes followed you around the room. It was a real canvas, though, not on velvet.

At that time Fredericton was split into three worlds: the university people, the people of the town, and the cultured society. Perhaps that's not quite fair, but that's how it seemed to us.

The cultured society had a Hammond organ put in the Gallery and a lady played quiet music on Sundays. Before we came, this conventional, stuffy attitude towards art was balanced by a vital little whirlwind of a woman, Lucy Jarvis, who ran the Art Centre at the University of New Brunswick. She and Pegi Nichol McLeod, I believe, had begun this centre sometime after the war — or perhaps during it as Pegi painted sailors and other service people for the war records, although she was not in the forces herself. I once met her in Ottawa and loved her explosive watercolours. Anyway, Lucy gathered a group of people around her who shared her vitality all through the 1950s and it was hard for us to follow in her footsteps, so we didn't try. She was a special person at a special time, and change was inevitable. And, of course, changes came to Fredericton, too. Now I wish that progress would stop, and no more malls or subdivisions would take over yet another wild place where mushrooms and Canada lilies once grew.

By Christmastime of that year of our arrival, we were so established and enthusiastic about New Brunswick, we hoped we'd never have to leave. Bruno's appointment as artist-in-residence was only for one year, so we decided to go back to England and Norway after the term ended in May. We went ahead with our plans, but Colin McKay told us we could come back and Bruno could run the art centre and have a studio on the campus as well.

FALL DAISIES

There are so many varieties of daisies — from the small ones with pink edges that grow in lawns, to wild daisies that cover the meadows and roadsides of New Brunswick, to tall Michaelmas daisies. My friend Reg Balch grows these beside his dark ravine at the back of his garden.

90

MOLLY LAMB B

Interlude

In London we rented a house in Cleaver Square, which is in Kensington on the north side of the Thames near Lambeth Bridge. It used to be a working people's neighbourhood, but the professionals had moved in and installed central heat and avocado doors with brass knockers. There was a pub at one end of the square and the London City and Guilds' Art School on the other. Bruno went to the School to draw from the model and I to learn about lithography.

The lithography teacher liked shooting pheasants more than teaching, so he was seldom in the studio. Another student, a big bear of a man, helped me quite a lot, lifting the heavy stones to the press and so on. His name was George Gordienko. He was quiet and reserved but I noticed he had a Canadian accent. He told me he came from Winnipeg. Soon we became friendly and I asked him to come home to lunch and have a glass of beer with Bruno. It became a regular habit, and one day he asked if we liked wrestling.

"No," I said bluntly. But Bruno said he did.

"I've a couple of tickets to a match. I'll give them to you, if you like," said George.

How modest he was. The tickets were for Albert Hall, and George was the star wrestler of the evening!

For me that was the beginning of a long series of canvasses about crowds. We'd go to a pub and George would have a neat scotch before his wrestling match. Bruno and I would sit in the crowd and wait for the show to begin. One chilly night in an outdoor ring in Folkstone, George had to fight a Russian. The crowd, of course, was on George's side. The two put on a violent enough show, but at one point they were locked together for a long time – too long for a woman sitting behind me.

"Oy," she shouted, "Come on, then, why don't you get married and make something of it?"

After the match we had supper with the Russian, who had a thick Cockney accent and came from Balham, a suburb of London.

That was a good summer. We remained friends with George and have stayed with him for many summers in Streatham. He bought a house there and rented parts of it to wrestler friends—all gentle men. Big John de Silva, the handsome Maori; Bernie from the north of England who had to rely on being funny in the ring because he wasn't much of a wrestler; Frank, an Australian who was past his prime and had so few bouts he read meters for a living and was keen on ballroom dancing.

Grey Street

Sometime in the 1960s we bought a house on Grey Street and it was our first gesture of permanence. We had, however, left all our furniture (that Bruno had made) in Vancouver and had to start from scratch. We found a second-hand store on King Street where we could buy all sorts of things for five or six dollars apiece. It was before antiques became so popular, so we filled our place with spool beds and dressers which only had to be scraped of their old layers of paint to look attractive. Pine boxes, brown earthenware jugs, pine tables, and 1910 kitchen chairs. We bought the chairs one day in Saint John—four of them for eight dollars. Bruno bargained with the man because one of the chairs had a broken rung.

"Seven dollars," said Bruno.

"Eight," said the man, "All you need to do is put the clamps to her."

My friend Emmy Sloat who lives on a farm near Keswick Ridge wouldn't give you a cent for our treasures. She grew up with these simple and beautiful things and now she has all the latest plastic. Her daughter even has a built-in vacuum cleaner.

It was good to have our own house. The attic became my studio. There was an oil stove in the kitchen and we made delicious, slow-cooking soups—oxtail and pea. In the fall we made jams and jellies and pickles—Lady Ashburnham pickle—ah, that's a great one.

When Lady Ashburnham was young she ran the telephone exchange at Stanley, so they say, and married Lord Ashburnham who must have been a remittance man from England. Years later she kindly donated her pickle recipe to a collection being got together by a group of ladies in Fredericton. Now I make her pickle every year and am full of gratitude.

We had lots of visitors on Grey Street, and once A.Y. Jackson came to stay for a whole week. He drove down here with his old friend, a Mr. Burton, I think his name was. It rained a lot that week and it was probably the last trip Jackson took before his stroke. Although I loved him, he made me very tired. He nodded off from time to time all day long, but stayed up until two or three in the morning. He was deaf and I spent so much time shouting at him. But we had some fine times, too. I took him to the farmer's market on Saturday morning and, amazingly, he was recognized. A woman who sold flowers gave him a bouquet and he loved that.

My old friend Herbie Webber, who had brought us pastrami sandwiches when we first arrived here, had a store on Queen Street then. He sold records and musical instruments, but also had a coffee bar. I took A.Y. there just before noon on a wet morning. Herbie was busy; the store was crowded. We came to the counter and when Herbie looked up from making out a bill I said smugly, excitedly, "Herbie, I'd like you to meet A.Y. Jackson."

There was a stunned silence. Then Herbie wrung A.Y.'s hand and said, "Free coffee all around!" A stockbroker called Bill Fink came rushing up and shook A.Y.'s hand, too, and said, "Just wait till I tell Ruby I met you, Dr. Jackson."

That was the last time I saw Uncle Alex well and happy. Later I went to Kleinburg, just outside Toronto, and visited him once or twice, but it wasn't the same. Just before he died, my friend Mary Lou and I visited him in a nursing home near Kleinburg, and I was allowed into his room. A nurse was feeding him his dinner. Chips, that's what he was eating, holding them in his stiff, arthritic fingers. His hands had been like that for as long as I could remember—he held his paint brushes the same way. I went to him and said, "Hi, Uncle Alex, remember me?"

"Huh," he said.

I yelled, "Remember Molly?"

"Huh," he said, "Of course I remember Molly," and fell to eating his chips again, and so I went away.

Our neighbours, kitty corner from us on Grey Street, were Ellen and Nan Gregg. Ellen had been a schoolteacher in St. Stephen before she retired, if you could call it retiring. She was still busy giving correspondence courses to prisoners at St. Vincent de Paul. One man carried on a long philosophical communication with her about whether or not there was a God. Nan, her sister, was a librarian at the University and she had acquired a very personal collection of paintings. Their house was like them. Nan's paintings, Ellen's letters—not only from prisoners, but so many from her old students. She must have been a great teacher. Both she and Nan were non-judges—and that's rare. Ellen also made quilts and still does.

Sometimes when walking by their house in winter with the dog, I can see Ellen under the Tiffany lamp, sewing little hexagonal pieces of cotton together. Ellen uses traditional New Brunswick designs for her quilts—Grandmother's Garden, The Fan. I don't remember the rest of the names but once I traded her a painting for two quilts.

A few years ago a Japanese lady came to Fredericton from Tokyo to visit her son who was a brilliant classicist here at the University. He was busy all the time with his work; she didn't speak much English, and it wasn't much fun for her at first. Once I took her fiddleheading on the river and she loved it. She walked daintily along the bank and everytime she found a fiddlehead she'd give a tinkle of a laugh and say, "So happy!"

Ellen knew Taruko—that was her name—had time on her hands and asked her if she would like to make quilts. Before you knew it, she was making one after the other with great skill and pleasure. Ellen sent the designs up to Williamsburg, where the women of the church finished them, and Taruko liked quilting so much that when she went back to Tokyo she kept right on sewing quilts and sending them back to be finished at Williamsburg. Eventually she branched out into her own Japanese designs – gun metal greys, whites, and earth browns. Tokyo is mad for them. Taruko has had a show – a big exhibition, in fact – and she is in all the leading newspapers and magazines. Just the other day I saw a clipping from a Tokyo newspaper which, of course, is in Japanese – except the words Nan, Ellen Gregg, and Williamsburg. I find things like these so surprising – like finding mushrooms or flowers in a way, only better because it's to do with people and chance meetings.

Three years ago we moved to a big old house just a block away from our first one on Grey. It's on Lansdowne, where we began seventeen years ago. Anny is off seeking her fortune in Vancouver. Sasha lives here in Fredericton some of the time, and I am working on a series which I called "The Queen Comes to New Brunswick."

"The Queen Comes to New Brunswick" show opened on September 27, 1977, and was for me as a painter the most satisfying evening because everyone came to see it – from the Premier to the girl who cuts my hair. And since the whole town had witnessed the event last summer, they were all able to respond to the canvasses on the walls – whatever their views or beliefs on painting.

Postscript

The Gleason Arms, St. Andrews, October 1977.

I am in a hotel like no other. Where else could you smell pickles being made in the kitchen? I have a front room, very old, and when I go to bed the lights of Water Street shine on the window panes.

It's quiet here at this time of year. The tourists have almost all gone. It rained last night and the leaves are falling and sticking to the pavement.

My dog Bertha and I have already developed a routine. We get up at dawn and walk along the beach behind the Gleason Arms. There's a little pale moon on its side, high in the sky and a green light at the end of the pier. No one on the beach at all, except us and a few seagulls. We come back to the hotel and I make breakfast in a little kitchen just outside my room. Then I get down to my writing. At ten we go out again. The sun shines on the juicy caramel seaweed at low tide. We walk out to the reef; Bertha chases the gulls and a lone heron. The wind is brisk and I've bought a Cowichan Indian tuque to keep my ears warm.

I cannot imagine a more beautiful life. I do love the Gleasons. Mr. Gleason has a barber shop and cut my hair for nothing yesterday. Mrs. Gleason gave me a bottle of the pickle she was making and told me of another place I could walk to, so Bertha and I went to the top of the town and found the trail. It wandered through a damp glade — silver fireweeds, willows, the smell of autumn leaves decaying — then over the railway tracks and up a field — red maple trees, rose hips, oaks, and an old russet apple almost at the top. The path ended by a chimney — the remains of a farmhouse — and beyond it was the sea which surrounds everything.

Coming home we walked another way and came to a field near a tidal swamp and a weir out in the water. It was so covered with white mushrooms that it reminded me of a crowded graveyard I once saw coming into New York from Idlewild Airport. Like a greedy eater at a feast too huge to devour, I filled my basket with the firmest and finest and walked back to the hotel along the beach.